KILLING AMERICA

Harrison House

Shippensburg, PA

ENDORSEMENTS

Gene and Teri Bailey's book, *Killing America*, is a practical and sometimes blunt account of how we as a nation got here, and what we must do to hold on to the America we love! This is not a time for the faint of heart. Lady Liberty is still standing, but some within our own borders want to destroy her. Get your copy of *Killing America* today, to find out how we can preserve all that we cherish!

Donald Trump Jr.

There is no doubt anymore. Americans are in a fight for the soul of America. Never before have we seen such corruption so pervasive in business, medicine, and yes, even in the highest offices in the land. Stolen elections, gender mutilations, and drag queens teaching our children once seemed like a really bad movie. However, today, we are living out that reality.

In these pages, Gene and Teri Bailey break down what happened, how it happened, and then give us practical steps of hope to bring America back to her place on the world stage. This nation is like no other. It has been often quoted, "Where America goes, so goes the world." Dive into this book and take your place as we all drive back the tsunami of darkness.

Kari Lake
America First Political Leader

Killing America is a must-read for patriots committed to saving America. Early in the book, Gene and Teri Bailey ask a provocative question: "If we are praying for America's rescue, wouldn't it be God's will to assign us each duties in this great spiritual struggle?"

The answer is "yes." Gene and Teri present a plethora of worthy tasks to be taken up by every member of God's team, and each reader is then faced with a choice: How will you respond to God's call on your life?

This book isn't for the weekend warrior; it is a book directed at those who desire to be rewarded in God's eternal Kingdom with rubies, diamonds, and crowns. If you want to store up your treasure in heaven and press into the will of Jesus our Savior now, this is your book.

I guarantee if you read this book the Holy Spirit will convict you and then use you. What a glorious prospect! To serve God in our given assignment is an honor beyond comprehension.

Floyd Brown
Founder, *Western Journal*

Gene and Teri are at the forefront of the cultural battle, and their book *Killing America* offers inspiration and direction for us to be the change needed for the church to align with heaven's plans and purposes.

David J. Harris Jr.
Author, Speaker
Host of *The David J. Harris Jr. Show*

In Gene and Teri's book *Killing America,* they remind us that, as a nation, despite our sin, we have been blessed because we are one nation under God. It is time that we, the people, rise up and, just like Isaac, dig again the wells of our covenant with God. We must come together, put aside our complacency, and stand up for what is right by making our voices heard.

Read this book and learn how to take a stand for our nation. Become familiar with your biblical and constitutional rights. Read it through once, and then again. Study it very carefully.

Thank you, Gene and Teri!

JESUS IS LORD!

Reverend Kenneth Copeland
Author, Founder of Kenneth Copeland Ministries
and the Victory Channel

Plain. Direct. Straightforward and simple. That is the approach Gene and Teri Bailey have taken in their book titled *Killing America.* They provide us with a comprehensive and crystal-clear update on the serious issues our nation is currently facing. And thankfully, they reveal the practical and scriptural steps to what it will take to save America.

As a Christian, a pastor, a citizen, a leader, a husband, father and grandfather, their book has inspired me to courageously stand up for America in an even greater way than I have before. Pastors, I encourage you to use this book as a reference guide for your sermons. Become familiar with the problems we face. Use the Scriptures and illustrations in the book. Then, stand up in your pulpit and boldly proclaim that "Jesus is STILL Lord over the United States of America!"

Pastor George Pearsons
Eagle Mountain International Church
(Gene and Teri's pastor!)

When Nehemiah heard of Jerusalem's devastation, he "wept and mourned for days" (Nehemiah 1:2-4). This mourning continued for several months as God imparted His broken heart to this faithful man. When the process was complete, the Lord began downloading a vision for rebuilding Jerusalem to Nehemiah. Only those who truly carry God's heart can be entrusted with His favor. This has been the process worked by Holy Spirit in Gene and Teri Bailey.

As you read this book, you'll realize immediately that they carry God's hurting heart for our beloved and devastated nation. You will also discover that, like Nehemiah, they have hope and strategy. Gene and Teri are two of America's modern-day reformers, full of faith-filled plans to rebuild the walls and see America restored. Please read and share this great book!

Dr. Dutch Sheets
Give Him 15

Gene and Teri Bailey's latest book, *Killing America,* is a clarion call to those who are not willing to lose hope in America but fight for her rights. Gene and Teri are clear in their concerns about where America is currently, but convey with sincerity how our nation can rise out of chaos and be stronger than ever. I encourage you to get your copy and let this powerful message incite your own passion to make a difference.

Joni Lamb
Daystar Television Network

One would have to be blind to not see the onslaught of darkness trying to destroy the United States of America. However, it takes another eye to see that so much of what is happening is intentional, and it's being furthered by groups that are bent upon the utmost forms of evil and who are determined to further a globalist agenda. When the epiphany of what is happening hits you, it makes you pause and reflect. From there, you begin to ponder about how you can personally get involved to interrupt it all.

In *Killing America,* Gene and Teri Bailey detail, in an unfiltered fashion, what is really happening in our country—but they don't share this critical information without offering hope! They reveal that with the Lord's help, there is always hope and that this country has been, and still is the catalyst for the Gospel being preached around the world. This book offers real solutions and ways that each of us, in our own spheres of influence, can disrupt the plans of darkness and ensure that the powers of evil cannot kill America! Every Christian and every person who truly cares about our nation must have this important message in their arsenal!

Pastors Hank and **Brenda Kunneman**
Lord of Hosts Church and One Voice Ministries
Omaha, Nebraska

Bold as lions and with the wisdom of the men of Issachar, Gene and Teri explain the times and more importantly, lay out a plan of action for what to do! This book is for anyone seeking to make sense of these troubled times and find genuine hope for restoring the "city on a hill."

Rick Green

Founder, Patriot Academy

The Gospel of Jesus provides an answer and solution for every single dilemma that we face. It is vital that we understand the issues at hand and remember that we do not battle against flesh and blood (Ephesians 6:12). Instead, we must stay connected to the heart of God in prayer. Having said that, I am so thankful for people like Gene and Teri Bailey, who are willing to back up their prayers with a courageous stand. In *Killing America,* we are provided with insight and strategy on how to restore our country to biblical values. This is our mandate for the nation of America and beyond—to partner with Him to see the reality of heaven displayed on Earth.

Bill Johnson

Bethel Church, Redding, California

Author of *Open Heavens* and *Experience the Impossible*

What a phenomenal book! *Killing America* by Gene and Teri Bailey is filled with great insight, information, and revelation that has not only the power to change your life but also our great nation. You need to get this book, read it, and then read it again—and by all means, share it!

The chapter Called to Occupy really resonated with me because, as Christians, that is what we are called to do by Jesus himself, "Occupy till I come." I was also struck by the quote from Frederick Douglas, "Where there is no struggle there is no progress." Read that again! Let me tell you something: we need to get out in the streets, if that's what it takes, to change this nation back to its roots, back to the way it was designed, back to the America we know and love. But the only way we're going to "turn back the tsunami of darkness" is if we all come together in one mind and one accord.

Friend, no matter what you see or hear going on in the world and in this great nation of ours, I have good news for you—all hope is not lost, and this great book confirms that. So, sit down and enjoy this good read because when you finish, you will *know* what to do!

Dr. Jesse Duplantis
Evangelist, Author, TV Host
President and Founder of Jesse Duplantis Ministries

No matter which way we look, our culture has come to an Isaiah 5:20 period in time when people are calling evil "good" and light "darkness." In the face of such darkness, it is time for God's people to roll up their sleeves and rise to the occasion. Gene and Teri Bailey are issuing a wake-up call that Christians all across America desperately need to hear. I highly recommend this timely book for everyone who wants a fresh infusion of hope for the future.

Dr. Ché Ahn
Senior Leader Harvest Rock Church, Pasadena, Calif.
President, Harvest International Ministry International
Chancellor, Wagner University

"Wow" is all I could say after reading Gene and Teri Bailey's new book, *Killing America.* This is a hard-hitting book in which Gene and Teri waste no words, spare no punches, and state very clearly the way things are and what must happen for things to be turned around. I promise that you will not be bored, not even for a second, as you read this book. It will provoke you to seek what role you must play to help turn things around so the killing of America is stopped.

Rick Renner
Minister, Author, Broadcaster
Moscow, Russia

In a culture inundated by fear and confusion, now more than ever, we need bold and courageous leadership in the body of Christ. Gene and Teri Bailey are just those leaders. While most have been lulled to sleep in a spiritual state of silence and complacency, they have taken a rare and unyielding stand for truth. I'm continually inspired by their love for God, love for people, and love for our nation. In their new book *Killing America,* Gene and Teri clearly expose the enemy's attempts to destroy America as they bring simple, practical solutions to how each of us can take a stand and make a difference. I want to honor the character and integrity of the Baileys and celebrate them as they release this very timely book!

Landon Schott
Senior Lead Pastor
Mercy Culture Church

KILLING AMERICA

TURNING THE TIDE ON THE TSUNAMI OF DARKNESS

GENE & TERI BAILEY

2nd Edition

All emphasis within Scripture quotations is the authors' own. Take note that the name satan and related names are not capitalized. We choose not to acknowledge him, even to the point of violating grammatical rules.

Published by Harrison House Publishers
Shippensburg, PA 17257

ISBN 13 TP: 978-1-6675-0345-5

ISBN 13 eBook: 978-1-6675-0346-2

For Worldwide Distribution, Printed in the USA

2 3 4 5 6 7 8 / 28 27 26 25 24

CONTENTS

FOREWORD

If you've ever watched my radio show or seen me speak, you know that I have a problem with a lot of Christian pastors. In one word, they're cowards.

Wisdom begins with the fear of the Lord—so says the book of Proverbs. But today's Christian leaders fear a great many things besides God. They fear condemnation from the press, from their neighbors, or from their own parishioners. They fear for their reputations. They fear being regarded as something other than respectable "good citizens." They fear death, instead of what comes after it.

And so, rather than speaking out, they go silent. They avoid speaking about controversial topics from the pulpit, or anywhere else. Instead of proclaiming the Gospel, they keep it half-hidden, presenting only the parts that are easy. They preach a private Christianity instead of a bold public one. Above all, they shun anything that is "too political," as if politics is entirely outside the realm of Christian values.

Fortunately, Gene and Teri Bailey are not that type of Christian. I've known both of them for years, long enough to know they are both the real thing. They know that the lives we live right now are only a prelude and that all of us will be judged for how we act today. They know that if we really believe in Christ and the Bible, then we need to publicly stand up for the unborn, for real marriage, for freedom of worship, and more.

They also aren't in denial about the challenge facing America. For 200 years, every American lived in a country that, whatever its flaws, was at least implicitly Christian in nature. The biblical worldview was taken for granted as the guidepost to live our lives by. That biblical worldview is what drove the Americans first to seek independence from Britain, then to abolish slavery. Because it strove to observe Christian ethics, America was blessed.

But for decades now, America has been turning away from that worldview. Gene and Teri can both tell you the result of that: Because we have abandoned God, terrible afflictions are coming for this country. Our freedoms have eroded, as has our wealth. Young Americans live confused lives of uncertainty and moral anarchy. The family is vanishing. Parents mutilate their children to win approval on social media. To quote Solzhenitsyn: "People have forgotten God, and that is why all these terrible things have happened."

But fortunately, Gene and Teri have a plan. They are experts on America's many past religious revivals, and they know how to pave the way for another one. "Killing America" may have a bleak title, but it's not a tale of despair. It's a road map for all who yearn to see America restored to her God-given glory. The Baileys' strategic guide offers actionable steps for every Christian who wishes to stand up for their values, while protecting their families from the tribulations to come and ensuring that their faith emerges intact on the other side.

As the Baileys so aptly remind us, we are not mere bystanders in this epic tale. We are active participants, chosen for this moment to make a difference. We shouldn't lament that we were born in a difficult time. We should rejoice that God has given us this chance to show our devotion.

America's story is a Christian story, one of resilience, redemption, and revival. With your help, America's next chapter won't be one of final collapse, but of its greatest-ever triumph.

Charlie Kirk

FOREWORD

I can hardly say how excited I am that Gene and Teri Bailey have written this vitally important book! Let's just say "very." That will give you the general idea. It has given me genuine joy to read it, and to know that many others can read it too.

First of all, I should mention that the book in your hands is very readable—which is not always the case with other books that are equally vitally important. I aspire in all the books I've written to be as readable as possible, because if a book doesn't pull the reader along to continue reading, it might as well not exist, no matter what important information it contains.

But just as important as being readable, this is a book filled with genuine hope. It is also filled with wisdom and truth and a raft of important information about exactly where we are in this country, so I would highly recommend it just for that.

But the idea that it is also filled with hope is what sets it apart. Without a clear sense of where God is in all that is happening, and of how he wants to lead us through this mess, it can all be depressing. But when you know it is his will to give us hope amidst the madness, it changes everything.

Only when you have real hope and know what God's will is can you really face what is happening in our nation. Without knowing that God has a real plan to turn it around—and desires to use us to do that—it really is easier simply to look away. Most of us can hardly believe what's happening in our great country, because it's unlike anything any of us ever dreamt could happen, certainly in our lifetimes. And because it's so horrifying it's much much easier for us to ignore it, to simply pretend it's not happening, or perhaps to tell ourselves it's at least not as bad as it seems. But when you see where God is in the middle of it all, everything changes.

So if you or anyone you know is tempted to despair because of all that we are seeing around us, you have in this book what I see as the antidote to that despair. We really do need to know that God himself desires to give us hope, so that we might give others hope—and so that we might all faithfully and joyfully join the fight to turn the tide of evil rising around us, by his grace. And when you understand what God is doing in the midst of the craziness, you won't just have hope, but will be drawn to be part of what he is doing, which is of course his plan.

So the gigantic question of whether this can all be turned around has a lot to do with you and whether you answer God's call to do your part in turning it around. Each of us has a vital role, and I believe this book will inspire you to play the specific role God has appointed for you and no one else.

I'm truly amazed to think that just a few years ago I didn't know who Gene and Teri Bailey were. The simple fact that God has in the midst of all the craziness of the last few years given us the Victory Channel and Flashpoint and Gene and Teri seems to me to be solid, incontrovertible evidence that God is not done with this country. He is raising up all kinds of people to give us hope, and to show us that we aren't the only ones who see what is happening and who want to be part of God's plan to do something about it.

Before I go, I should mention one more important thing. Gene Bailey is genuinely funny. Which is actually important. I have a bunch of worldly "funny" credentials. In college I edited the Yale humor magazine and before I was born-again I had an ambition to write for David Letterman and SNL and Jerry Seinfeld, and almost did. After I became a Christian—but before all the mainstream publications like the New York Times went plum loco in shilling for the dark side—I used to write humorous things for them and for similar publications that have also gone over to the dark side. But the point is that anyone who knows me knows how seriously I take humor.

But one of the reasons I take it so seriously is because I know it's one of the main ways God helps us to communicate effectively. It's also one of the things that enables us to exhibit God's joy in the midst of all that troubles us. So when I say that Gene is genuinely funny, it's about more than just being funny—and making fun of me when I appear on Flashpoint! It's about communicating clearly and it's about the joy of the Lord. That all by itself is one of the reasons I'm so glad he and Teri are in my lives today, and in the lives of everyone who is aware of their important ministry.

So read this book they've written and share it and spread the hope and the joy that God wants us all to experience and share. And may God bless you as you do so!

Eric Metaxas
New York City
October 2023

1

KILLING AMERICA

Look, it's no secret. We all know what's going down. We've been suffering through it together for quite a while now. But things seem to be escalating. They're getting out of hand, and worse than we could have possibly imagined. It's hard to wrap our minds around some of the things we're watching unfold before our eyes. The forces of the dark agendas determined to bring this country to extinction and extinguish the flame of freedom have been at work for several generations. They have attempted to dismantle this great "experiment in freedom," that has been a beacon of hope to the world for more than 200 years. There is no easy way to describe it. No feel-good clichés. Our great nation is in trouble—deep trouble.

Our blessed America, the land of the free and home of the brave, the place of dreams and opportunities, of baseball, Chevrolet, and apple pie—the country we love—is being killed. When we say "killed," we mean those behind this dark agenda will stop at nothing less than the absolute demise of America as we know it. This one nation, under God, raised up by God, founded on Judeo-Christian values as a bastion of light and a defender of the weak, is being murdered in cold blood.

We realize that "murdered in cold blood" is extremely harsh verbiage that might cause many to cringe and think it might be an overstatement. But we believe it's an accurate description of what's happening. Any plot to destroy this God-given nation is evil.

When the beacon of freedom that is America is taken out of the picture and the world suddenly becomes a much darker place, the hope of freedom for the oppressed in other nations begins to fade, and the threat of tyranny can begin to move into that vacuum. Founding father Thomas Paine wrote in his famous 1776 pamphlet *Common Sense*, "The cause of America is in a great measure the cause of all mankind."[1]

Is America perfect? Certainly not. Do we have issues? Most definitely. We've made many mistakes and blunders and certainly had our dark moments. However, America has had a solid history of picking herself up, engaging in rigorous debate, correcting her mistakes, and preserving freedom and liberty.

The founding fathers set up our republic with a system of checks and balances because they were fully aware of the evil and deceptive tendencies of human nature. The ones who want to kill America are set on eliminating those checks and balances. On September 18, 1787, at the Constitutional Convention that met in Philadelphia, Dr. Benjamin Franklin was asked, "Doctor, what have we got? A republic or a monarchy?" He replied, "A republic, if you can keep it."[2] Later, we'll explain the difference between a republic and a democracy, but Franklin understood all too well that going forward, opposing forces with outright evil intentions would be coming to take America out.

Nevertheless, God's hand has been on our republic, and we've managed to keep it, though it's been an endless fight throughout our history. America is still, without question, the greatest nation on the planet. Indian-American political commentator, author, and filmmaker Dinesh D'Souza said it well, "America is the greatest, freest and most decent society in existence. It is an oasis of goodness in a desert of cynicism and barbarism. This country, once an experiment unique in the world, is now the last best hope for the world."[3]

You have to ask yourself, why else would millions flood to our border, risking their lives to get in? Why would fathers and mothers in third-world countries send their children away on the harrowing, life-threatening journeys through jungles, mountains and bloodthirsty cartels? Simple.

Because America gives them hope.

America remains the world's most generous nation, sending more aid to hurting countries and more military support against tyrannical regimes than any other. A free America is what stands in the way of a total global world order. Not to mention, we still train and support financially, and send out more missionaries to spread the Gospel than any other country in the world.

Plus, America has consistently stood with Israel since its inception in May 1948, even known as Israel's big brother. Numbers 24:9 in the Bible says, "Whoever blesses Israel will be blessed, and whoever curses Israel will be cursed" (Good News Translation). Yes, we have been blessed, but things have been shifting. God's hand has been on our nation, but we are now on the verge of being "cursed."

THEY ARE KILLING AMERICA

America is not being assassinated with a quick bullet to the head, or even being overtaken suddenly by foreign militaries. Bombs aren't being dropped, and missiles aren't flying—not yet, anyway. Instead, it seems our country is suffering a slow, painful death by poisoning. What makes it even more deplorable is the ones who appear to be administering the toxic doses are from within our own ranks.

Over the years, it seems we've allowed subversion from the American ideal set by our founding fathers. For decades, we've ignorantly and numbly watched the gradual execution while occupied on our rabbit-eared TVs with fuzzy screens, which transitioned into Technicolor on our RCA TVs, and advanced on to high-definition, flat screens and smartphones. All the while we were eating our popcorn and cheering our favorite sports teams.

Sure, from time to time, we would get concerned, have moments of uneasiness, but then we'd go back to being distracted and pacified by our toys and comforts. All the while, our freedoms were being stripped away, ever so subtly, as lethal ideologies were slowly injected into our culture.

Germaine Copeland, bestselling author of the Prayers That Avail Much book series with more than seven million copies sold,[4] told us, "Over 50 years ago, I heard a former Communist youth leader outline the plan to take over our nation. She said they were already in important positions in the media, universities, government, etc. I may have been the only one who walked out that day believing her. Everyone I talked with, or attempted to tell, said it will never happen in America."

Eventually, the deadly venom started taking its toll, to the point where it appears our Lady Liberty is now gasping from its cumulative effects. The closer she is to death, the weaker she becomes and the more accelerated the damage. The forces against her saw an opportunity to finish her off and sent a tsunami of darkness to drown her in depravity. It's a double whammy—a poisoning by deadly ideology, so far from the strength of our original biblical Judeo-Christian values, and drowning by a tsunami of its dark outgrowth.

This is where we find ourselves, in what appears to be the last stages: shallow breathing and possible signs of a death rattle is near. Meanwhile, the tide of darkness seems to be rising. Make no mistake. The forces of darkness are not out to merely change America and make her over by implementing their own progressive agenda. They want America as we know it, destroyed, including your freedoms, so something entirely new and extremely dark can be ushered in.

Total control appears to be the goal. Logical dialogue is not in the playbook, so First Amendment rights seem to be heavily targeted. The old adage: "I respect your views and you respect mine," is not part of the agenda. "I allow you to be your own person, but I don't agree with you," is apparently not acceptable, either.

The key here is that often disagreement is labeled "hate speech." It seems if we don't affirm and celebrate others' ungodliness, we're guilty of hate speech. Labeling our freedoms as "hate speech" provides the moral license to marginalize and then tyrannize. Because we can't be shut down with a logical argument, we will be shut down by belittling or laughing at us.[5] Or, we may be screamed over so we can't be heard, maybe even shoved, punched in the face or knocked to the floor. Property is sometimes destroyed, and cities burned.[6]

If we're fortunate, we won't be beaten, hospitalized or possibly arrested. Yes, arrested, because the whole time, during the ordeal, there is an insistence that we need to be kind. We are blamed as the ones actually provoking the violence and bullying them because of our disagreement with their ideologies.[7]

You and I are, in essence, being fed to the lions while our antagonists sit in the colosseum cheering. In Roman times, thousands packed an arena to laugh and cheer while Christians were ripped apart and eaten by lions. The general public had been desensitized while Christians were dehumanized and deemed a threat to a pagan society. Humans are capable of doing horrible things. Jeremiah 17:9 (KJV) says: "The heart is deceitful above all things, and desperately wicked: who can know it?"

Today, if you are a patriot, a conservative, or want to see America turn back to her original foundation of Judeo-Christian values, you find yourself in the minority. If you love this country, you are considered by many a racist, bigot or even a hater worthy of being fed to the lions.

America is a God-given nation and her documents of freedom are based on biblical values. What we are affirming is America is a space for freedom of worship, freedom of speech, freedom of thought and to pursue life, liberty and happiness. It was founded on godly principles (that we will look at throughout this book).

PURE INSANITY

David Jeremiah wrote a book titled, *I Never Thought I'd See the Day.*[8] We can relate, except we'd probably title it: "Never in Our Wildest Imaginings Would We Have Believed." The dark mindset attempting to dominate our culture seems intent on purposely dismantling biblical values set up by God since creation. The attack on marriage instituted by God (Genesis 2:21-24) has attempted to dismantle His design for the family unit of a biological male father, a biological female mother and the biological or adopted offspring produced by their union.

The father's leadership over many years, has often been ridiculed[9] and the mother's role redefined.[10] Non-biblical viewpoints have been taught in our educational systems on all levels. With both parents working outside the home in most American households and so many children being relegated to long hours in daycare, often little attention is paid to what is going on in children's daily schooling. Many parents have been, for the most part, uninvolved and trusting that their children are receiving the basic education they expect of a system with agendas far different from the reading, writing and 'rithmetic of years gone by.

Authorities leading children's education in their districts, counties and states, in whom the parents' trust was placed, have taught their offspring the theory of evolution instead of God, the creator, taken the Ten Commandments off school and any civic property and forbidden even their sports coaches to say silent prayers at the end of sports events.

Without a knowledge or acknowledgment of God, and educators forbidden to speak of Him in the classroom, and in the absence of a spiritual anchor, many children are experiencing depression, anxiety and often despair.[11]

Just a small development to perhaps distance students even further from discovering the truth of our Judeo-Christian heritage occurred in 2010 when a decision was made in the development of the Common Core State Standards Initiative, embraced by 41 of our 50 states, to not include cursive writing in school curriculums. An article in *Education Week* says, "One of the most widely cited criticisms of the Common Core State Standards is that they don't require teaching students to write in cursive."[12] Why would that kind of decision be made? It might seem like a harmless shift since nearly everything is done on computers and phones these days, right? But we should be asking "why?" about everything in our lives in our current world.

The same article says:

> Proponents of teaching cursive say students need to learn it to be able to read historical documents, such as the U.S. Constitution. Without knowing cursive, students "will be locked out of doing research with literary papers and archival collections," Valerie Hotchkiss, a library director at the University of Illinois at Urbana-Champaign, wrote in the *Chronicle of Higher Education* in 2014. "They will not even

> be able to read their grandmother's diary or their parents' love letters."[13]

Is it possible that removing cursive from the curriculum has been done purposely to keep upcoming generations from reading the originals of America's founding documents which show the basic values on which our country was founded? Just something to think about. It all adds up to the creation of a tsunami of darkness. But being ignorant of the depth and devotion of the agenda to bring down our nation, we let it happen.

But it's a lot worse than we thought.

We have been ignorant and, even if many suspected something wasn't quite right, were hesitant or unwilling to get involved. But, the whole time, the proponents of the dark agendas have been strategic. The darkest agendas, blatantly against biblical values, are often openly celebrated as good, while true biblical goodness is often vilified as the worst type of evil. The Bible cautions: "Woe unto them that call evil good, and good evil" (Isaiah 5:20 KJV). "Woe," according to God's book, is not a good place to be, yet it seems this is where our nation is being pushed.

Part of "woe" is being turned over by God to a debased mind. "And even as they did not like to retain God in their knowledge, God gave them over to a debased mind, to do those things which are not fitting" (Romans 1:28 NKJV). Other translations say a "reprobate" or "depraved" mind. Whichever translation you use, the verdict is clear. This explains why we are seeing such widespread depravity.

For example, transgenders and crossdressers, often called "drag queens," are being encouraged to go into some public elementary schools and libraries across the U.S. at taxpayer's expense, where they are celebrated as "normal."[14] Elementary school-aged children are being exposed to and influenced by the LGBTQIA+ community and presented their lifestyles as they read stories to children that foster those lifestyles.[15] In January 2023, in Renton, Washington, a cross-dresser, "After kicking off her presentation with books about Santa [and his husband] and snowball fights, Sylvia O'Stayformore led the song with a shout: 'If you're a drag queen and you know it, blow a kiss!'"[16] Again, keep in mind these events are often funded by tax dollars and grants that are hard at work against your and your family's values. By not taking the time to speak against these things, we are complacent toward the killing of America.

Gender confusion and reassignment is on the rise in the U.S. and Europe, according to the *British Medical Journal*[17] along with affirming alternative sexual orientations. Some school counselors, persuaded of the importance of affirming students' desires to identify as other than their biological sex have sometimes even become enemies to the parents, encouraging children to go with their desire to identify as gay, lesbian, asexual, non-binary, etc.[18] In some states, if an underage child thinks they are transgender and the parents do not agree, some children have been removed from the home.[19] In public high schools these days, being straight is considered boring, while bi, gay, or trans is cool.

If you are like us, you have become aware of a group of people who identify as animals called furries. In Oklahoma, that could prove to be risky. Representative Justin Humphrey has introduced a bill that, if passed, furries could be collected by animal control. Parents would have to go to the pound to pick up their children who believe in anthropomorphic behavior.[20]

This anti-biblical values continue, with many political leaders choosing to go against clear evidence-based science and God's natural order, by refusing to define and accept biological males and females as God's ordained creation. Biological males identifying as women threaten women's sports. These transgender males have often been celebrated.

Disney has become strongly committed to LGBTQIA+ inclusiveness at their theme parks and movie productions.[21] Bud Light put a transgender's photo on their beer cans and, as a result, lost billions of dollars.[22] Target included products from an "overtly-satanic, radical LGBTQIA+ supplier," for so-called "pride month" in 2022.[23] Also, if you were out shopping months after "pride month," you would have found many of their "pride" products in the deeply-discounted sections.

Let's face it, the majority of us are finished with all of this.

We would remind you that "pride" is one thing that God cannot stomach. The Scriptures are pretty straightforward with how God feels about it. "To fear the Lord is to hate evil; I hate pride and arrogance, evil behavior and perverse speech" (Proverbs 8:13 NIV). The gay and LGBTQIA+ lifestyle is essentially like shaking a fist at God the creator who "created them male and female"—only two genders. Stealing the rainbow, God's symbol of promise, and turning it into a symbol of their lifestyle underscores how far our society has fallen away from our foundational biblical values.

As we wrote this chapter, a large gathering of LGBTQIA+ activists and families were invited to the White House where they listened to a speech affirming their lifestyle. In the background, an LGBTQIA+ rainbow flag was hung between two American flags from the White House portico. Right on the White House South Lawn, some of the activists were topless, displaying a new level of disrespect and decadence for the White House and what it stands for.[24]

Though his comment pertained to another, unrelated national incident, former Fox News commentator, Tucker Carlson, said something very telling about the events and cultural shifts occurring in our nation: "What was once considered admirable is now derided as stupid, if not racist—that would include achievement, intelligence, honesty, self-control, humility. Those are features of the old America; those were yesterday's virtues, they are gone. In their place, all that we once considered contemptible and repulsive—we're told to worship that now."[25]

This is not our America.

Some say, "What's the big deal? Let people be people. I do my thing, you do yours." The big deal is it cuts to the core of God's creative order. We are looking at the redefinition of the whole human race, the bedrock of the family with the redefinition of marriage—in essence, pushing out the God of creation and His divine design for mankind. This is serious.

What's even more serious is many are complacent as we witness the seeming use of transgenderism and LGBTQIA to LGBTQIA+ as a tool for political gain. By the way, LGBTQIA+ stands for lesbian, gay, bisexual, transgender, queer or questioning, intersex, and asexual. The "+" stands for gender fluidity, or however you feel you identify. There are 107 gender identities in the United States that were listed for 2023.

The same is true with the woke culture. Yet what is going on is about much more than transgender ideology and alternative lifestyles. Those are merely symptoms of a much deeper issue. That deeper issue goes all the way back to taking God out of our schools and government and devaluing human life by embracing abortion. The more we embrace anti-biblical ideologies, the more reprobate we become and the more depraved the results. The all-out assaults on America in an attempt to kill her are extensive.

The following are just a few more:

- The politicization and weaponization of Covid, the lockdowns and Covid vaccines.[26] It was only the beginning. Something more sinister is in the making. Rumors of another Covid outbreak complete with masks, vaccines, lockdowns, and more are seemingly lurking.[27]
- Inciting racial wars.[28] Heritage.org states: "Critical Race Theory (CRT) makes race the prism through which its proponents analyze all aspects of American life—and do so with a degree of persistence that has helped CRT impact all of American life."
- Threats to our Second Amendment rights.[29] Allowing out of control crime, shoplifting and looting,[30] defunding the police, and depicting them as evil.[31]

- It seems mainstream media is reprogramming American minds. News and social media seem to control the narrative and what people think to turn elections.
- Open borders.[32] In addition to illegal aliens, many of whom are gang criminals and drug smugglers, fentanyl is flooding across our open borders,[33] killing hundreds of thousands of our citizens, mostly kids, annually.[34] It seems the societal assault of this drug is a direct attempt from our enemies to kill America from within.
- Elections. What was once considered a conspiracy theory continues to prove correct. Recently, 10,000 mail-in ballots were discovered in a Pennsylvania election.[35]
- Do you know what country is one of the largest consumers of human trafficking? You guessed it, good old U.S. of A. Kind of explains why we have open borders and so many unescorted young children coming across our border.[36]

These are only some, but you get the grim picture.

Imagine where we will be in five years if we don't make our voices heard and fight back.

They are killing America.

That is the bad news. The good news is, there is still *hope*. America is not dead yet!

NOTES

1. Thomas Paine, *Common Sense* (London: H.D. Symonds, 1776), Thomas Paine Society; https://www.thomaspainesociety.org/common-sense; accessed April 19, 2024.
2. Julie Miller, "'A republic if you can keep it': Elizabeth Willing Powel, Benjamin Franklin, and the James McHenry Journal," *Library of Congress Blogs,* January 6, 2022; https://blogs.loc.gov/manuscripts/2022/01/a-republic-if-you-can-keep-it-elizabeth-willing-powel-benjamin-franklin-and-the-james-mchenry-journal/; accessed April 19, 2024.
3. Dinesh D'Souza, *What's So Great about America* (Washington, DC: Regnery Publishing, 2002), 193.
4. Germaine Copeland, *Prayers That Avail Much,* Twenty-fifth edition (Tulsa, OK: Harrison House Publishers, 2005).
5. Saul Alinsky, *Rules for Radicals* (New York: Vintage Books/Penguin Random House, 1989); "RULE 5: Ridicule is man's most potent weapon. There is no defense. It's irrational. It's infuriating. It also works as a key pressure point to force the enemy into concessions."
6. Ibid., "RULE 3: "Whenever possible, go outside the expertise of the enemy. Look for ways to increase insecurity, anxiety, and uncertainty."
7. Ibid., "RULE 10: "If you push a negative hard enough, it will push through and become a positive. Violence from the other side can win the public to your side because the public sympathizes with the underdog."
8. David Jeremiah, *I Never Thought I'd See the Day* (Nashville: FaithWords, 2012).

9. Erica Scherrer, "Why Are Sitcom Dads Still So Inept?" *The Conversation,* June 16, 2020; https://theconversation.com/why-are-sitcom-dads-still-so-inept-139737; accessed April 19, 2024.

10. "The Foster's Review: Remarkably Frank, Overtly Liberal, Yet Great," *Denver Post,* April 29, 2016; https://www.denverpost.com/2013/07/29/the-fosters-review-remarkably-frank-overtly-liberal-yet-great/; accessed April 19, 2024.

11. "New HHS Study in JAMA Pediatrics Shows Significant Increases in Children Diagnosed with Mental Health Conditions From 2016 to 2020, *U.S. Department of Health and Human Services,* March 14, 2022; https://www.hhs.gov/about/news/2022/03/14/new-hhs-study-jama-pediatrics-shows-significant-increases-children-diagnosed-mental-health-conditions-2016-2020.html; accessed April 19, 2024.

12. Liana Loewus, "Why Don't the Common-Core Standards Include Cursive Writing?" *Education Week,* October 10, 2016; https://www.edweek.org/teaching-learning/why-dont-the-common-core-standards-include-cursive-writing/2016/10; accessed April 19, 2024.

13. Ibid.

14. Alison Flood, "Protest seeks to stop US libraries supporting Drag Queen Story Hour," *The Guardian*, August 7, 2019; https://www.theguardian.com/books/2019/aug/07/protes and-seeks-to-stop-us-libraries-supporting-drag-queen-story-hour; Tim Fitzsimons, "Drag Queen Story Hour brings pride and glamor to libraries across the U.S.," *NBC News,* July 2018; https://www.nbcnews.com/feature/nbc-out/drag-queen-story-hour-brings-pride-glamor-libraries-across-u-n884671; both articles accessed April 19, 2024.

15. "Drag Queen Story Hour Brings Pride and Glamor to Libraries Across the US…, NBC News July 2018.Ibid.
16. Jaweed Kaleem, "How drag queen story hour became a battle over gender, sexuality and kids," *Los Angeles Times,* February 22, 2023; https://www.latimes.com/world-nation/story/2023-02-22/drag-queen-story-hour; accessed April 19, 2024.
17. "Gender dysphoria is rising—and so is professional disagreement," *BMJ (British Medical Journal)* Newsroom; https://www.bmj.com/company/newsroom/gender-dysphoria-in-young-people-is-rising-and-so-is-professional-disagreement/; accessed April 19, 2024.
18. Kelsy Bolar, "School Affirms 11-Year-Old's Trans Identity Without Parental Consent," *Independent Women's Forum;* https://www.iwf.org/identity-crisis-stories/jennifer/; accessed April 19, 2024.
19. Emilie Kao, "Pelosi's Equality Act Could Leas to More Parents Losing Custody of Kids Who Want 'Gender Transition,'" *The Heritage Foundation,* January 15, 2019; https://www.heritage.org/marriage-and-family/commentary/pelosis-equality-act-could-lead-more-parents-losing-custody-kids-who; accessed April 19, 2024.
20. Alexia Aston, "Oklahoma lawmaker targeting 'flurries' in schools: Who is Justin Humphrey?" *The Oklahoman,* January 18, 2024; https://www.oklahoman.com/story/news/politics/2024/01/18/who-is-justin-humphrey-oklahoma-furry-bill-departure-from-lawmakers-history/72266697007/; accessed April 19, 2024.
21. Brooks Barnes, "GLAAD Praises Increased Inclusiveness of Disney Films," *The New York Times*, December 15, 2022; https://www.nytimes.com/2022/12/15/business/media/glaad-disney-lgbtq.html; accessed April 19, 2024.

22. Kat Tenbarge, "Transgender influencer Dylan Mulvaney says Bud Light never reached out to her after backlash," *NBC News,* June 29, 2023; https://www.nbcnews.com/nbc-out/trans-influencer-dylan-mulvaney-responds-bud-light-backlash-rcna91899; accessed April 19, 2024.

23. "Target Reeling From LGBTQ Clothing Line Backlash," *Decision Magazine,* May 31, 2023; https://decisionmagazine.com/target-reeling-from-lgbtq-clothing-line-uproar/; accessed April 19, 2024.

24. "Transgender Activists No Longer Welcome at White House After Going Topless at a Biden Event," *AP Washington News,* June 13, 2023; https://apnews.com/article/biden-transgender-topless-white-house-rose-montoya-811dc7f4473ad6b3dd43dbec7f8b5d37; accessed April 19, 2024.

25. Kevin Haggerty, "Tucker takes a flamethrower to Hunter Biden after sweetheart deal, torches KJP too," *American Wire,* June 21, 2023; https://americanwirenews.com/tucker-takes-a-flamethrower-to-hunter-biden-after-sweetheart-deal-torches-kjp-too/; accessed April 19, 2024.

26. P. Sol Hart, Sedona Chinn, Stuart Soroka, "Politicization and Polarization in COVID-19 in News Coverage," *NIH, National Library of Medicine,* October 2020; https://www.ncbi.nlm.nih.gov/pmc/articles/PMC7447862/; accessed April 19, 2024.

27. John Bell, "The next pandemic is coming—and the world isn't ready," *The Independent, US Edition,* April 16, 2023; https://www.independent.co.uk/voices/pandemic-covid-prepare-pathogens-future-b2315593.html; accessed April 19, 2024. And Sheila Mulrooney Eldred, "9 diseases that keep epidemiologists up at night," *NPR,* January 29, 2023; https://www.npr.org/sections/goatsands

oda/2023/01/29/1151039454/9-diseases-virus-epidemiologists-pandemic-potential-who; both accessed April 19, 2024.

28. Jonathan Butcher and Mike Gonzalez, "Critical Race Theory, the New Intolerance, and Its Grip on America, The Heritage Foundation, December 7, 2020; https://www.heritage.org/civil-rights/report/critical-race-theory-the-new-intolerance-and-its-grip-america; accessed April 19, 2024.

29. "Major Threats to the Second Amendment," The Essential Second Amendment, *heritage.org,* https://www.heritage.org/the-essential-second-amendment/major-threats-the-second-amendment; accessed April 19, 2024.

30. Lee Ohanian, "Why Shoplifting Is Now DeFacto Legal In California," *Hoover Institution,* August 3, 2021; https://www.hoover.org/research/why-shoplifting-now-de-facto-legal-california; accessed April 29, 2024.

31. Senator John Thune, "Demonizing and Defunding Police Has Consequences," U.S. Senator, South Dakota website Op-Ed, July 16, 2021; https://www.thune.senate.gov/public/index.cfm/2021/7/demonizing-and-defunding-police-has-consequences; accessed April 19, 2024.

32. Victoria Coates and Lora Ries, "Biden Wants Open Borders All the Way South to Guatemala," *The Heritage Foundation,* December 5, 2023; https://www.heritage.org/immigration/commentary/biden-wants-open-borders-all-the-way-south-guatemala; accessed April 19, 2024.

33. "Chairman Green: 'Every Dollar the Cartels Rake in Comes at a Cost of An American Life or Livelihood,'" opening remarks in full committee hearing on Secretary Mayorkas' loss of operational control to cartels, July 19, 2023; https://homeland.house.gov/2023/07/19/

chairman-green-every-dollar-the-cartels-rake-in-comes-at-the-cost-of-an-american-life-or-livelihood/; accessed April 19, 2024.

34. Aimee Cunningham, "Fentanyl deaths have spiked among U.S. children and teens," *Science News,* April 28, 2023; https://www.sciencenews.org/article/fentanyl-deaths-children-teens-opioid; accessed April 19, 2024.
35. Hannah Nightingale, "Chicago Board of Elections finds 10,000 missing ballots in Dem DA primary race after 'tabulation' error," *PM.,* March 25, 2024; https://thepostmillennial.com/chicago-board-of-elections-finds-10000-missing-ballots-in-dem-da-primary-race-after-tabulation-error; accessed April 19, 2024.
36. "Child Trafficking by Country 2024," *World Population Review;* https://worldpopulationreview.com/country-rankings/child-trafficking-by-country; accessed April 19, 2024.

2

AN OPPORTUNITY TO HOPE

This is a unique way to start a chapter, but we wanted to use an illustration from the movie "Evan Almighty." Perhaps you've seen it. In it, Evan is a newly elected congressman whose campaign officially declares that he will change the world. Evan asks God to give him the opportunity to fulfill his declaration. The problem is, Evan wants to change the world his way, using his own methods. God, however, has something completely different in mind. God wants to change Evan's plan to His plan and methods.

So God, played by actor Morgan Freeman, pays Evan a visit and reveals what He wants Evan to do. Initially, Evan thinks the old man is a nutcase; but after some supernatural displays, he's convinced and reluctantly accepts his peculiar assignment.

Evan soon discovers that even though it's a God assignment, it's not easy. Since taking up the divine mission, he is being made fun of and portrayed as a fool by the media, kind of like our country is being portrayed as a fool by the media. This is not only hard on Evan, but on his wife, Joan, as well. She also had prayed to God, except it was to bring her marriage and family closer. There's a scene in which Joan goes into a restaurant for lunch and, unbeknown to her, God, again played by Morgan Freeman, is serving her.

God is warm and inviting, so Joan opens up. Not knowing she's talking to God, Joan tells Him who her media-bashed husband is and his eccentric assignment. Of course, God already knows. As she's explaining her plight, you can feel the tension all of this has created in their marriage. She skeptically admits, "My husband says God told him to do it," and then asks, "What do you do with that?"

God's answer is profound. "Sounds like an opportunity," he responds. "Let me ask you something. If someone prays for patience, do you think God gives them patience or gives them the opportunity to be patient? If you prayed for courage, does God give them courage or give them an opportunity to be courageous? If someone prays for the family to be closer, do you think God zaps them with warm fuzzy feelings, or does He give them opportunities to love each other?"

Just as Evan prayed to change the world and Joan prayed for her marriage and family, we have asked God to expose the evil and corruption plaguing of our nation. We prayed for God to raise up leaders who would bring us back to and rebuild our original constitutional foundation. We believe He is doing that. It's just that we had no idea how deeply perverse and corrupt everything really was.

★ ★

It takes some time to expose all the toxins that need to be forever removed before renovating. Is it some aspects of the Church, the FBI, the CIA, the media, Disney, Target, other major companies? We're not sure, but we're finding out. It's all part of the process. His process. His plan. And it's our opportunity to step up.

When someone buys a fixer-upper building, they usually start by ripping down the walls, ceiling, and flooring. When they do, sometimes during the process, uh-oh, they discover mold. At that point, do they just continue with the remodeling and put up the new? No. They start by gutting the old structure and then de-molding it. When they do finally install the new, it will be the latest and greatest materials, with safeguards put into place to prevent the mold from ever having a possibility of reappearing.

We're here to say hope is not lost. America has been turned around before with God's help, and with His help she will be turned around again. The trouble is, we live in an instant society that demands millisecond answers to complex questions Googled on our latest, fastest upgrade. We want to avoid discomfort or work. Let's just plug our destination into the GPS, hop on over to the express lane, avoid the crashes, and find the easiest and quickest possible route with the least amount of effort and sacrifice.

We prayed and asked God for help, yet we want to tell Him how He should save us, by whom, and how fast. But please don't ask us to get involved. We have too much on our plates, important stuff. We want patience and courage, as Morgan Freeman said, but we just don't want to take on the mantle that opportunity requires.

To revive our Lady Liberty, it's going to take more—from us. Everybody has a role to play. Even seemingly small roles are significant. Don't be intimidated into apathy thinking you're a nobody. God delights in using everyday people like us. Someone once said, "God has a habit of picking up nobodies and making them somebodies." It's true. We simply have to be available.

Even though the dire condition of our nation screams for us to give in to despair, we serve the God of miracles and revivals. He can empower us to stop this tsunami of darkness and actually produce a tsunami of light and righteousness throughout our nation. We can change the landscape permanently for good. Sometimes it takes a tsunami to stop a tsunami, but it's going to take a tsunami wave of people like us stepping out of the bleachers and getting into the game.

We must have some skin in the game. It's like a teenager who gets a brand-new, expensive sports car from his parents. On his first week out, he shows off and crashes, totaling the car. The parents are thankful their son is alive and hopefully has learned a valuable lesson. A bit wiser, they now make the boy hitch rides for a while, then let him start working for his own car. By the sweat of his brow, he finally saves enough to purchase a used, borderline junker. He cleans it, waxes it, and cares for it like it's a $130,000 Corvette. Now, he has some skin in the game.

Similarly, God allows us to get some skin in the game. A lot of us, however, have more than skin in the game. We have deep cuts, bruises and broken bones that have come from our own government that was supposed to protect us. All we have to say is, most people know that the most ferocious kind of animal to deal with is a wounded one. Well, multitudes of us are wounded and ready to stand up, stand strong and get into the game.

THE ROOT OF OUR PROBLEM

What is our hope? Here it is. First, this is not meant to be an overtly spiritual book, yet the reality of the situation at the root of our problem is deeply spiritual. There is simply no avoiding it, and it impacts all of us, believers in God or not. As you will see later, even unbelievers benefit with more freedom when there is spiritual freedom.

Of course, our adversaries bark the opposite, but they are missing the mark. Proverbs couldn't be any clearer: "When the righteous are in authority, the people rejoice: but when the wicked beareth rule, the people mourn" (Proverbs 29:2 KJV). The word "righteous" here in the Hebrew is *tsadeq*, which means "to be just or righteous," including the government. There is a just and godly way to exercise government, and there is a wicked way.

When the righteous are in leadership, there is liberty. When the wicked rule, instead of freedom there is tyranny and the labeling of good as evil and evil as good. We seem to be witnessing the latter. It appears the evil-desired endgame is total control and manipulation. Matthew Henry wrote in his commentary about this Scripture in Proverbs 29:2, "The people have cause to rejoice or mourn, as their rulers are righteous or wicked. Righteous men walk in liberty, and walk in safety. The scornful mock at things sacred and serious. Men who promote religion, which is true wisdom, turn away the wrath of God."[1]

We think it's safe to say that the entities trying to kill America scornfully mock things sacred and serious, while pushing for legislation that celebrates overt wickedness. One example is the Drag Queen Sisters of Perpetual Indulgence who mock holiness, while doing vile acts dressed in drag as nuns.[2]

This doesn't mean a righteous leader has to be particularly religious, but that he or she is governing by godly principles. Some leaders, for example, may or may not be spiritual people, but might be pro-freedom of religion, speech, the Second Amendment, and other freedoms we hold dear as Americans. Policies that are supported more often than not lined up with the Judeo-Christian worldview on which this nation was founded. Some even supported Israel.

Throughout the Bible, God used secular leaders to protect and promote His people. Think of Nehemiah. A trusted cupbearer to the king, he heard his hometown of Jerusalem was in trouble because of broken-down walls. He cried out to God, and instead of saying, "I'm just a cupbearer," he said, "Lord, send me." This ordinary man stepped up to lead the rebuilding of the Jerusalem wall and accomplished in 52 days what others couldn't do in years.

America is desperate for Nehemiahs. What is not talked about much, however, is that Nehemiah's funding, backing, and military protection came from a secular leader, King Artaxerxes

I. As those like Nehemiah begin to step up, the wrath of God can be turned away from America and freedom will reign. Yes, this is a spiritual problem requiring spiritual warfare that manifests in practical actions and solutions.

The apostle Paul wrote, "For we do not wrestle against flesh and blood, but against principalities, against powers, against the rulers of the darkness of this age, against spiritual hosts of wickedness in the heavenly places" (Ephesians 6:12 NKJV). There are principalities and hordes of demonic spirits that are attempting to dismantle America's righteous foundation and destroy her God-given identity. Our battle, first and foremost, is not against people; but as the Bible says, is against evil principalities and powers.

Another Scripture says, "For the weapons of our warfare are not carnal but mighty in God for pulling down strongholds, casting down arguments and every high thing that exalts itself against the knowledge of God, bringing every thought into captivity to the obedience of Christ" (2 Corinthians 10:4-5 NKJV).

In the Old Testament, Daniel, like Nehemiah, was in deep mourning about the state and future of his nation. He had fasted and prayed for three weeks when an angel appeared to him in a vision and said, "Since the first day that you set your mind to gain understanding and to humble yourself before your God, your words were heard, and I have come in response to them. But the prince of the Persian kingdom resisted me twenty-one days. Then Michael, one of the chief princes, came to help me, because I was detained there with the king of Persia" (Daniel 10:12-13 NIV).

What's amazing about this passage is it gives a peek into the activity of principalities and powers. Ellicott's Bible Commentary on Daniel 10:13 says, "Perhaps no single verse in the whole of the Scriptures speaks more clearly than this upon the invisible powers which rule and influence nations."[3] The spiritual realities have not changed. There is an evil entity behind the evil that is set on killing America. How else can you explain the overt depravity in the face of God? But God's hand was on our establishment of our covenant, nation and America is part of God's divine plan. This is why the warfare has been so intense. Why do we believe that? There are many reasons written in our history and founding documents.

To start with, on April 29, 1607, Robert Hunt landed on a beach in Virginia that we now call Cape Henry. He instructed the landing party to cut out a portion of the ship's beams from the hull. Notice the commitment level here. Cutting pieces out of the hull of your ship is not exactly a good thing to do, yet they did it. The landing party then took those timbers, erected a cross, and drove it into the beachhead proclaiming this land for Christ, king and country.

Those in positions of greatest power today are using language that is diametrically opposed to our nation's foundational intentions to promote a socialist, anti-God worldview. Our cries for revival may seem to be drowned out by the loud evil agendas of hatred and control, but we know that God heard Robert Hunt and his men on that day, as they declared this nation belonged to the Lord. God took them seriously and hasn't forgotten.

The Mayflower Compact of 1620 and The Declaration of Independence in 1776 further reiterate that we are a people who have sought to follow God. Following are some direct quotes from these founding documents.

The Mayflower Compact was a set of rules for self-governance established by the English settlers who traveled across the Atlantic Ocean to the New World on the Mayflower. Throughout the short document, it's obvious that the intention was to establish a nation based on Christian values. The document opens with, "In the name of God, Amen." It continues with, "…by the Grace of God…Having undertaken, for the Glory of God, and Advancement of the Christian Faith…in the Presence of God, and one another, covenant and combine ourselves together into a civil Body Politick, for our better Ordering and Preservation, and Furtherance of the Ends aforesaid…."[4]

A later journal, with several authors, is a report of the voyage and first year of the settlement at Plymouth, called Mourt's Relation. John Robinson, pastor to the Pilgrims while they were still in Holland before their journey, provided the model for the Mayflower Compact and was one of the leaders in planning for the journey. He was also a religious contributor and legal justifier of the colony described in Mourt's Relation.[5] He counseled the Pilgrims to choose as leaders those who, "diligently promote the common good," and not to "begrudge in them the ordinariness of their persons, but God's ordinance for your good."[6]

When the 13 states of America finally decided to break away from Great Britain, The Declaration of Independence was written. The Revolutionary War helped complete the final break from Britain and birth of the new, independent nation. It was to be established on the founder's core beliefs: "We hold these truths to be self-evident, that all men are created equal, that they are endowed by their Creator with certain unalienable Rights, that among these are Life, Liberty and the pursuit of Happiness." Life, liberty, and the pursuit of happiness all come from the Creator.

Throughout history, everywhere that "no God" was promoted, tyranny and oppression followed. Why is it that throughout modern history, whenever totalitarian governments invaded a nation, almost always the first thing they did was confiscate Bibles and imprison or kill Christians and Jews? It's because God's enemy knows that true freedom and liberty come from God. You can't control people who know they are "endowed by their Creator with certain inalienable Rights."

In the opening paragraph of The Declaration of Independence, we find the words, "the separate and equal station to which the Laws of Nature and of Nature's God entitle them." This is important because the Bible tells us in Romans 2:14-15 that the Gentiles, who did not have God's written law, by *nature* did the things prescribed by the law of God. And it shows the law of God is written on the human heart.

Part of the genius in the founding of America was it was based on natural law. The Declaration of Independence declared "these truths to be self-evident" because all of us are made in the image of God and we have the law of God written on our hearts. For instance, everybody knows internally that men and women are different, that it's wrong to lie, to cheat, and to slander. It's wrong to commit murder, and so on. That's natural law.

So it's quite clear what our founding fathers had in mind as they established our beloved nation. This is why those who are out to kill America want to rewrite our founding documents. China is currently rewriting the Bible and teaching it in their schools.[7] As we pen this chapter, there is a massive effort by the progressives to change the Constitution, and it is gaining support.

This brings to mind former California Governor Ronald Reagan's famous inaugural address January 5, 1967. He spoke of our foundation of freedom: "Perhaps you and I have lived too long with this miracle to properly be appreciative," Reagan cautioned. "Freedom," he continued, "is a fragile thing and it's never more than one generation away from extinction. It is not ours by way of inheritance; it must be fought for and defended constantly by each generation, for it comes only once to a people. And those in world history who have known freedom and then lost it have never known it again."[8] Let those last few words sink in: "those in world history who have known freedom and then lost it have never known it again."

Despite this sobering fact, many Americans today, including countless elected officials, have lost the gravity of the founding documents and the godly principles that our nation was established upon. This is critical because the core principle of every one of those documents is freedom.

But know this. God is not in a panic. He's very much at work. He is for America and is not trying to come up with a response to the evil that has been unleashed in her. He's cleansing the mold. Long before this chaos began, God was already positioning His Nehemiahs and Davids and Mordecais and Esthers for such a time as this. God has always had a remnant of praying people whose hearts He has gripped, who've taken their place working with Holy Spirit to see that America stayed in alignment with His purposes.

God's redemptive plan for America is already set in motion; and as we respond to opportunities to step up and take our places, we will see His plan get the best of the enemy's schemes. The enemy of our souls has schemes, but we are not unaware, "in order that Satan might not outwit us. For we are not unaware of his schemes" (2 Corinthians 2:11 NIV).

Though it sometimes seems like evil is winning, it's not too late. For sure, it will take standing in faith, trusting God, and a lot of wrestling in spiritual warfare, but we can wrestle control in prayer back from the administrators of darkness. Understand, however, spiritual warfare is more than being locked in our prayer closets. That's important, but engaging in spiritual warfare more often than not results in practical physical actions, steps, and assignments. What happens in the spiritual realm establishes itself in the natural world (see James 2:20).

What we see now raging in our nation cannot be understood by mere carnal thinking, because it's not carnal. It's spiritual. It's about good and evil. Though evil is a reality, we don't have to be overcome by it. "Do not be overcome by evil," wrote Paul, "but overcome evil with good" (Romans 12:21 NIV). We overcome evil with good.

We must step up with good to replace the evil. This is not a time for weak-willed Christians who back down from truth. We have to be strong enough to not cave in to the pressure of the world around us. The local church is meant to be a training ground that gives us strength and equips us for what we're facing. Rock and roll legend Mylon LeFevre who later became a minister, told the story of being in Army boot camp and seeing some of the recruits daydreaming and even taking a nap during hand grenade training. Can you imagine? Napping during hand grenade training?

Well, in a similar fashion we've sat in church and listened to the Word of God preached for years, maybe daydreaming or napping, not realizing that the Word of God was our hand grenade for life-and-death situations like right now. We have to wake up from our slumber.

And we are waking up!

THE WATCHMEN DECREE

The following is a decree that we (Gene and Teri) wrote called The Watchmen Decree. It's for all of us:

> I attest my allegiance first and foremost to the kingdom of God in the Great Commission. Second, I agree to be a watchman over our nation concerning its people and their rights for life, liberty, and the pursuit of happiness; whereas we the church or God's governing body on the Earth; whereas we have been given legal power from heaven and now exercise our authority; whereas we are God's ambassadors and spokespeople over the Earth; whereas through the power of God we are the

world influencers; whereas because of our covenant with God we are equipped and delegated by Him to destroy every attempted advance of the enemy's, we make our declarations. Number one, we decree that America's executive branch of government will honor God and defend the Constitution. We decree that our legislative branch, Congress, will write only laws that are righteous and constitutional. We decree that our judicial system will issue rulings that are biblical and constitutional. We declare that we stand against wokeness, the occult in every evil attempt against our nation. We declare and we now take back our God-given freedoms according to our Constitution. We declare that we take back influence at the local level in our communities. We decree that we take back and permanently control positions of influence and leadership in each of the Nine Gates of Authority. We decree that the blood of Jesus covers and protects our nation. It protects and separates us for God. We declare that our nation is energy independent. We declare that America is strong spiritually, financially, militarily, medically and technologically. We decree that evil carries no power, authority or rights in our land nor over our people. We decree that we will operate in unity going beyond denominational lines in order to accomplish the purposes of God for our nation, and we decree that America shall be saved.

Yes. There is hope.

NOTES

1. Matthew Henry, *Concise Commentary on the Whole Bible*, Proverbs 29:2; https://biblehub.com/commentaries/proverbs/29-2.htm; accessed April 19, 2024.

2. Todd Starnes, "'They Mocked Christ on the Cross'—Catholics Outraged Over LA Dodgers," *ToddStarnes.com,* May 24, 2023; https://www.toddstarnes.com/crime/they-mocked-christ-on-the-cross-catholics-outraged-over-la-dodgers/; accessed April 29, 2024.

3. Daniel 10:13, *Ellicott's Commentary for English Readers*; https://biblehub.com/commentaries/ellicott/daniel/10.htm; accessed April 19, 2024.

4. "The Mayflower Compact," *The Mayflower Society,* https://themayflowersociety.org/history/the-mayflower-compact/; accessed April 19, 2024.

5. Joshua J. Mark, "Mourt's Relation," *World History Encyclopedia;* November 18, 2020; https://www.worldhistory.org/Mourt's_Relation/; accessed April 19, 2024.

6. Ibid.

7. Rep. Mike Gallagher, "The Chinese Communist Party is rewriting the Bible," *Fox News Opinion,* July 17, 2023; https://www.foxnews.com/opinion/chinese-communist-party-rewriting-bible; accessed April 19, 2024.

8. Ronald Reagan, "January 5, 1967: Inaugural Address," *Reagan Library,* https://www.reaganlibrary.gov/archives/speech/january-5-1967-inaugural-address-public-ceremony; accessed April 19, 2024.

3

THE FAÇADE

In 1991, about a year or so after the Berlin Wall fell, I (Gene) was sent to Russia by the Kenneth Copeland Ministries (KCM) to do some work for them alongside Rick Renner Ministries, who was based in Latvia at that time. The flight made a connection in Germany where I, along with two other guys with me, changed planes that flew us on to Latvia. At that point in time, Latvia had just come out from under Soviet occupation that had begun in 1940. I had no idea of the eye-opening experience that lay ahead of us.

Our plane touched down at an airport in Riga, Latvia, but instead of pulling up to the gate like occurs at most airports, it came to a stop right in the middle of the crude, potholed and cracked runway. In fact, there was no gate or building to pull up to at all, and it appeared there were no people around either. It seemed like it was just our jet sitting on an eroded landing strip surrounded by pasture and trees. One of the crew popped opened the door and put the ladder down. The pilot got out first, found our luggage, and tossed it on the ground.

Then, he hopped back in the plane and took off, leaving the three of us standing there looking around. I kid you not, the jet was full of people, and we were the only three passengers who got off. They basically dropped us off in the middle of the runway. And did I mention it was cold?

Then we noticed a dilapidated building that was the airport terminal. I'm sure there was some sort of radio communication inside, but it was not at all what you would expect. It was like going back in time to 1945. Remember, this was supposedly an international airport. We were flying in from Germany.

We hauled our exhausted bodies and luggage over to the falling apart building where a guy who didn't speak any English met us. He stamped our passports and said stuff we didn't understand. Finally, someone from Rick Renner's ministry came to pick us up. Rick Renner Ministries partnered with KCM, and God has used them to build an impactful ministry in Russia and around the world.

Today, Rick's television broadcasts has millions of potential viewers; they have seen several million people accept Christ. At one point, his ministry oversaw more than 800 churches and pastors throughout the former Soviet Union. Today Rick and his wife oversee the Moscow Good News Church with over 2,000 active members as well as other affiliates around Moscow and in other parts of the former Soviet Union.

Rick is the founder and overseer of the Internet Good News Church, a fully online church with more than 200,000 members worldwide who are Russian speakers. But of course, back in 1990 all of it was just a seed and a vision.

★ ★

For us three guys, the airport experience in Riga was just the beginning of a 14-day trip through Minsk, Belarus, then on to Lithuania and finally Moscow, including a dreadful midnight train ride into Moscow. The poor, depressed-looking passengers on board were impoverished beyond what most Americans could imagine. Plus, the trains back in those days were filthy and foul smelling with windows screwed down so passengers couldn't let any fresh air in or escape if you wanted to! The experience was dehumanizing.

This, along with the primitive airport we flew into, was the first of many shocks the trip would bring. Here was the great country of Russia we had seen in the media growing up. There were air raid drills in school when we hid under our desks because of what this USSR superpower may do. Yet the reality before me now was the opposite of a superpower. The country's infrastructure back in those days was crumbling and ruined. Extreme poverty was everywhere.

On the street, we even encountered people trying to sell us military hats and coats, even their uniforms for a couple of dollars because their dollar, the ruble, had fallen so far as to be worthless. It was horrible. On one hand, it was really sad; but on the other hand, we were like, "Wait a minute. This is the big con job because the country, portrayed as a superpower during the collapse of the USSR, is anything but. The military was weak and unmotivated."

Once we arrived in Moscow, we went to the famous Red Square. Having heard about it and seen pictures my whole life—then to be standing in the center of it was surreal. Another thing that shocked me, at that early moment when the USSR had just collapsed, were all the Christian missionaries from America speaking English. It was like a wave of good news flowing into a dry and thirsty land.

After the wall fell, Russia opened up to the Gospel and America faithfully sent her missionaries. When people's hearts are changed by the Gospel and Holy Spirit, a grassroots change begins to take place in society. Like we pointed out in Chapter 1, Lady Liberty still sends out more missionaries to spread the Gospel than any other nation on the planet. The United States sends roughly 135,000 long-term missionaries compared to Brazil, which is second with 40,000.[1] We believe this is one reason God continues to bless the U.S.A. and also why the enemy wants so desperately to kill us. Can you imagine the dark impact on the world if we were no longer able to send out missionaries?

Despite the presence of many missionaries, back in those days it still was an eerie feeling to be there in Russia. We could feel freedom suffocating away as the walls of communism closed in around us. There was an underlying spirit of fear among the people.

One unsettling aspect about Moscow was the city streets. It is well known in Moscow that there was once a prison below street level. No one knows exactly how big it is. Especially during Stalin's time, people went in there but many never came out. Back in those earlier times, it was common for a van to pull up on a city street in Moscow, grab someone, and that person was never heard from again.

During our visit, the spirit of fear was never more tangible than in our guide. He would tremble and then run away whenever a car drove near us that looked like a government official's car. I had never experienced fear being tangible among a group of people in a city like that. It was eye-opening because we have such personal freedom and security in America.

However, that same type of fear is trying to overtake us today. Creating an atmosphere of fear—whether through lockdowns, masks, global warming, or guns—has been another weapon used in the attempt to kill America. If they can keep us fearful, they can control us. However, the word of God tells us, "For God has not given us a spirit of fear, but of power and of love and of a sound mind" (2 Timothy 1:7 NKJV). This is another reason they hate the Bible and us.

Though the walls in Russia had come down and the gates opened, the devastating effects of the poisonous system clung to the people and culture like an infectious disease. My big takeaway lesson from my time there was how things can be portrayed as one way, when reality is completely different.

But now that the walls were down, we were able to go inside the Kremlin for a tour of the museums there. Once we crossed that gate into the inside of the giant courtyard of the Kremlin, suddenly the streets were paved as if we were in Northeastern Virginia. The trees were beautiful, the landscape manicured. Mercedes, BMWs, Cadillacs were everywhere. Yet just outside those walls, people's cars were in horrible condition, rusted, smoking Russian klunkers. The infrastructure was crumbling, and poverty abounded. It was all a façade. The media and propaganda machine had lied to us.

Here's something else significant I found out. From 1929 through 1953, Joseph Stalin tried desperately to squash religious freedom and conducted brutal campaigns against the Bible and the church. They shut down churches, confiscated Bibles, even killed and imprisoned Christians, especially leaders.

"Stalin saw this as a way of getting rid of a past that was holding people back, and marching towards the future of science and progress," says historian Steven Merritt Miner. Does that sound familiar? The reality is, however, instead of marching toward progress, "Stalin accelerated the violence and oppression of the Leninist period."[2] What's interesting is when Stalin made his speech, he was standing only feet away from a magnificent historical church that had honored saints buried there.

But Saint Basil's Cathedral was now merely a monument of a greater past. So it's one thing to say, "God is dead," but they weren't going to tear down the edifices they had built to honor all the great revivalists who had come through Russia centuries ago.

How does that work? How can they say God is dead over here, but 20 feet away from them is a stunning cathedral that could never be replaced. Those pillars of Christianity in Russia had been buried and memorialized even though the leaders, from Lenin to Stalin, all the way until before the wall came down, were declaring atheism as the state doctrine.

The era of Communist rule began in Russia in 1917 and Karl Marx, coauthor of "The Communist Manifesto," declared, "Communism begins where atheism begins." Socialism, Marxism, and Communism had ruled with great promise and fanfare.

Yet before me, I was seeing the brutal truth played out. It's a reality that the progressives in America want to ignore. It was an astounding experience to understand how a government could control religion and thus its people.

Similar to Stalin's declaration that "God is dead," on April 8, 1966, the cover of Time Magazine read, "Is God Dead?" The question was meant to be cynical. John T. Elson, who wrote the article, "framed his story as a clarion of 'the new atheism' of the 1960s, a testimony to a cultural crisis of faith in which the very premise of a personal God was coming undone."[3]

As we will see, the reality of Elson's statement has proven quite the opposite. Yet at the time, the progressive culture took the bait hook, line, and sinker. The "God is dead" philosophy, along with the socialist, communist, hate-America teachers, professors, and ideologues, began poisoning everything.

At the same time, Madalyn Murray O'Hair, the activist who founded the American Atheists organization in 1963, was instrumental in the Supreme Court's decision to take God and prayer out of the public schools. O'Hair is a testament to the powerful effect that one person can have both negatively and positively.

Yet despite all the anti-God, atheist takeover of our schools and government, God would have the last laugh. He's always moving, and there was a tsunami spiritual awakening called the Jesus Movement that swept the nation in the late 1960s and early '70s. It was a direct response to the anti-God rhetoric being force-fed down the country's throat.

The blockbuster movie "The Jesus Revolution" was based on part of it. Some even contend that the Jesus Movement revival actually saved America for the time being by turning away the threatening tsunami of darkness. What's wild—almost like God said, "Just watch me"—is that on June 21, 1971, just five years after Elson's cover and article saying, "Is God Dead?" the Time Magazine cover was "The Jesus Revolution" and that now famous article written by Stan Zagorski started out with the words, "JESUS CHRIST, ALIAS: THE MESSIAH, THE SON OF GOD, KING OF KINGS, LORD OF LORDS, PRINCE OF PEACE, ETC. ...WARNING: HE IS STILL AT LARGE! He is indeed."[4] The article went on to note that the revival:

> Cuts across nearly all the social dividing lines, from crew cut to long hair, right to left, rich to poor. It shows considerable staying power... It has been powerful enough to divert many young people from serious drug addiction.[5]
>
> Christian coffeehouses have opened in many cities, signaling their faith even in their names: The Way Word in Greenwich Village, the Catacombs in Seattle, I Am in Spokane. A strip joint has been converted to a "Christian nightclub" in San Antonio. Communal "Christian houses" are multiplying like loaves and fishes for youngsters hungry for homes, many reaching out to the troubled with round-the-clock telephone hot lines.[6]

Perhaps what we recently saw occur with what has now been labeled the Asbury Awakening is just the beginning of another tsunami revival. Consider this. From February 8, 2023, through February 24, 2023, approximately 15,000 people a day poured into the Hughes Auditorium simply to worship and cry out to God. By its end, the revival brought 50,000 to 70,000 visitors to Asbury University, representing more than 200 academic institutions and multiple countries. That has to have an impact on those institutions. It's supernatural what God can and will do.

The point to all this, again, is what those wanting to kill America are putting in front of us—the promises, the agendas, and answers they proclaim are all a façade just like Soviet Russia was a façade. Gender fluidity is a façade. A trans person may claim they are a certain gender, but the reality is in the biology.

While writing this book, it was announced that a woman transitioned to a man and then got pregnant. The media announced with great enthusiasm that "Man gives birth!" No. It's a façade. The reality is, a woman who thinks she's a man got pregnant and had a baby. The examples of this insanity are endless. We saw a "there are more than two genders" t-shirt with a rainbow behind those words. When you go to order the shirts, under fit type, you can select either men or women. Again, it's just nuts.

ECONOMIC CORRUPTION

Back in 1990 Russia, as I began to comprehend the insane level of corruption, I also started to understand that the average people in Russia up to that point all pretty much got paid the same amount. It sounds like a noble ideal, but it's as corrupt as can be and goes against God's "natural law" that our founding fathers recognized. I witnessed firsthand what it meant to live in a place where there was no free enterprise. There was no motivation to work harder because everybody got paid the same. The people were scrambling to make ends meet.

Yet just around the corner would be a magnificent estate for an elite. For example, when we were in Latvia, we passed this incredible palace, and I asked Rick Renner about it. He said, "This palace was built for Catherine the Great's boyfriend." I was like, "Her boyfriend?" I couldn't believe it. We're talking opulent wealth. But it just wasn't with the people. It was all held by those few at the top.

Those who want to kill America have a romantic ideal about equality, but it's an illusion, a façade. Proverbs 14:12 (NKJV) says, "There is a way that seems right to a man, but its end is the way of death." This is particularly true with the communist, socialist, and Marxist-infused philosophies that they want to take root in America. Our founding fathers understood this. That's why they wrote in the Constitution that men, "are endowed by their Creator with certain inalienable rights, that among these are Life, Liberty and the pursuit of Happiness. That to secure these rights, governments are instituted among men, deriving their just powers from the consent of the governed.... That whenever any form of Government becomes destructive of these ends, it is the Right of the People to alter or to abolish it." Let that sink in.

When the government becomes destructive toward life, liberty and the pursuit of happiness, "it is the Right of the People to alter or to abolish it."

We must rise up! It's our God-given, constitutional right.

WEST AFRICA

Another time I was in West Africa. I landed in Conakry, Guinea, looking for stories on missionaries for the Christian and Missionary Alliance denomination. We landed at night, slept, got up the next morning, and heard gunfire. The gunfire related to the airport workers who had not been paid, so they were staging a protest. The police and the municipal authorities chimed in and then the military realized, "Hey, this is going really well," so they decided to take over the country. That usually meant bad stuff for missionaries and their helpers.

So I had to hide out. I was wearing navy ripstop pants that are made for the jungle. I had my boots on. I was ready. I had to hide out for more than 10 days. We couldn't escape the country until the military left. They were shooting in the air, demolishing property, and killing people. I had family back home who had no clue what was going on. This was before email or cell phones. Americans had no idea what we lived through in Africa during this time, fleeing for our lives.

Getting a real-world view is something most Americans have no clue about. For example, we complain about gas prices while over there they are struggling to just get enough food to survive. These experiences helped adjust my worldview and realize that the lower class in America has opulent wealth compared to most nations in the world. Approximately 70 to 80 percent of the world is living in third-world conditions dominated by poverty, hunger, corruption and constrained freedoms.

While driving down the streets in Abidjan, Côte d'Ivoire (Ivory Coast in southern West Africa), I was flagged down by a policeman to pull over. He came up to my window and said, "How about some money?" He was asking for a bribe, didn't flinch or blink an eye. Just wanted money. Corruption has destroyed these countries.

Nigeria, for example, is one of the world's richest in natural resources.[7] The people there should be living very, very well. Instead, the corruption is so high that it's the exact opposite. While I was there, I saw the majority of the population living in squalor. It was like the streets of India. It was horrible. Here's a nation that has some of the richest minerals in the world, yet because of corruption it's an impoverished disaster.

Basically, what we're seeing now is an attempt to kill America and make it like these third-world countries where chaos, crime, and corruption rule, where we have no choice and no control over our lives. Just think of all the riots when property was destroyed, people walking down the street are blatantly assaulted by gangs, shoplifting mobs are so bad that stores have to shut down or move. Instead of being arrested and prosecuted, these criminals are being embraced and encouraged, while parents who simply voice their concerns at school board meetings are labeled terrorists and saying God created them male and female is considered hate speech. Get it? We think you do.

RE-DUG WELLS

In Genesis we read that Isaac re-dug the wells of his father, Abraham: "And Isaac dug again the wells of water which they had dug in the days of Abraham his father, for the Philistines had stopped them up after the death of Abraham. He called them by the names which his father had called them" (Genesis 26:18 NKJV). Why is this significant for us today? The Philistines, similar to the woke progressives in America, wanted to cover up the past and ignore the promises of God to Abraham and his seed. They filled the wells, sealed them off, and wanted to act like they and Abraham never existed.

This is what the enemy of our nation wants to do with our Constitution and founding documents. They want to cover them up like they never existed, even rewrite them depicting a different history. But what did Isaac do in the face of the Philistines? He re-dug those wells and named them as Abraham had. This action was met with hostility and hatred by the Philistines. Isaac re-dug the wells of water. The naming of wells by Abraham was the hereditary right of his family to the property. Closing off the wells by the Philistines was to obliterate the traces of their origin. Isaac re-dug them and restored the original names, which also proclaimed his divine rights.[8] As people who love God and America, we are called to be Isaacs. We can't let them destroy our history or our promises.

What we have before us is a history. A history of promise that leads to life, liberty and the pursuit of happiness—opposed to a world history that reveals the corruption of the ideologies being forced upon America and ultimately where they lead. All we have to do is look at the world around us to see that if we continue down this path, this is what our destiny is. We have a choice. Re-dig our wells that name our rights, or stick our heads in the ground and allow the enemy to lie to us and ultimately destroy us.

We have been a nation under covenant with God. That's the reason we've been different. That's why we are not like Russia or Africa or other third-world countries. God is the reason we've survived as long as we have despite everything that's going on now. We have had our godly foundation as a basis, and we still have a remnant fighting for God and His will in this country. They are Isaacs, re-digging our wells. Revival like in the 1960s and '70s is churning again. God is not done. It's coming at a cost of hostility and hatred, but like Isaac we have to keep digging. If America's freedoms die, the rest of the world gets even darker.

We have to remind people that's what makes us different. We have to say it out loud. We're not just talking about Marxism; we're talking blatant communism. It's like when people say marijuana is a gateway drug. Socialism leads to Marxism, which leads to communism. And the best prevention is not to go down that initial path. When we see them trying to make us godless, it's because that's where communism flourishes. You see them attacking the family because in our opinion, they want to take the children, and that's what they're doing in some states.

No free will, no choice is the standard they want, and they will weaponize whatever they can to make that happen—creating pandemics, lockdowns, forcing vaccines, election fraud, labeling any verbal opposition as hate speech and terrorism, creating race tensions, allowing illegal immigrants to flood in with violent criminals and fatal drugs, on and on. You know it's true.

A SERIOUS WARNING

When we talk about killing America, we must understand they are going right into our homes and backyards. They want our kids and grandkids. The psalmist wrote, "Children are a heritage from the Lord, offspring a reward from him. Like arrows in the hands of a warrior are children born in one's youth. Blessed is the man whose quiver is full of them. They will not be put to shame when they contend with their opponents in court" (Psalm 127:3-5 NIV). Our children are our wells. They are our arrows to protect us later. Godly children will "contend with their opponents in court." The New King James Version says, "But shall speak [confront] with their enemies in the gate." We need our children. They are our future, and the enemy knows this.

Our children are being aborted at alarming rates. They are taking away their innocence, trying to confuse their genders. If they can keep them confused, they can control them and eventually sterilize them.[9] No seed made in the image of God. It seems to us they're trying to pervert a generation so that they can flip our Christian heritage to replace God with government.

Adolf Hitler said, "He alone, who owns the youth, gains the future."[10] He understood that. The core of his Red Army and Brownshirts were indoctrinated youths. The Hitler Youth and the League of German Girls were developed as Nazi Party youth groups to indoctrinate children and juveniles to Nazi ideology and policy. These youth groups also prepared Germany's young people for unquestioning commitment in war.[11] This is a battle plan by those killing America, and it still is working. We're just waking up to it.

There was the false perception that this could never happen in America. We thought because we're a Christian nation and because we're Americans, we're good. We've had to grow up a lot in the last two or three years to understand, wait a minute, it can happen and is happening.

When in Russia back in 1992, I learned that at the time of the wall coming down one in four people was a KGB informant. Many were kids who were indoctrinated to tell on their parents. It was their duty to their mother nation if they saw their parents do something contrary, to report them. I met a wonderful man named Sasha, who was probably in his 30s but looked like he was in his mid-50s or 60s.

Life had been that hard. He was a Christian, and I asked him when did he get saved? "I got saved twelve years ago," he said. I then asked about his wife. He said, "Well I didn't tell my wife because I was concerned that she would turn me in, but I love my wife." That's how much fear controlled him. After the wall came down, he told his wife he had been saved and was a Christian. Come to find out she had been saved about a year later after he did. Think of it. For years, they had been living in the same house, both of them believers, yet living in so much fear they felt they couldn't tell each other.

We have to re-dig our wells and name them. We can't let them have our kids and families and kill America. We can't become like them.

NOTES

1. Gina A. Zurlo, Todd M. Johnson, and Peter F. Crossing, "World Christianity and Mission 2020: Ongoing Shift to the Global South," *International Bulletin of Mission Research,* 2020, Vol. 44 (1); https://journals.sagepub.com/doi/pdf/10.1177/2396939319880074; accessed April 20, 2024.
2. Steven Merritt Miner, *Stalin's Holy War: Religion, Nationalism, and Alliance Politics, 1941-1945* (Chapel Hill, NC: The University of North Carolina Press, 2003).
3. Leigh Eric Schmidt, "Is God Dead? A TIME Cover Turns 50," *Religion & Politics,* April 5, 2016; https://religionandpolitics.org/2016/04/05/is-god-dead-a-time-cover-turns-50/; accessed April 20, 2024.
4. Stan Zagorski, "The Alternative Jesus: Psychedelic Christ," *TIME,* June 21, 1971; https://content.time.com/time/subscriber/article/0,33009,905202,00.html; accessed April 20, 2024.
5. Ibid.
6. Ibid.
7. "Nigeria: extreme inequality in numbers," OXFAM International; https://www.oxfam.org/en/Nigeria-extreme-inequality-numbers; accessed April 20, 2024.

8. Robert Jamieson, A.R. Fausset and David Brown, *A Commentary, Critical, Practical, and Explanatory on the Old and New Testaments* (1882), Genesis 26:18, https://biblehub.com/commentaries/jfb/genesis/26.htm; accessed April 29, 2024.
9. Analisa Trofimuk, "Rep. Mary Miller says White House is encouraging kids to take "castration" drugs, undergo surgeries; PolitiFact, The Poynter Institute, April 17, 2022; https://www.politifact.com/factchecks/2022/apr/17/mary-miller/rep-mary-miller-says-white-house-encouraging-kids-/; accessed April 20, 2024.
10. Olivia B. Waxman, "Hitler Youth and the Real Nazi History...," October 17, 2019; https://time.com/5700753/hilter-youth-jojo-rabbit/; accessed April 20, 2024.
11. "Hitler Youth Nazi organization"; https://www.britannica.com/topic/Hitler-Youth; accessed April 20, 2024.

4

DRAWING THE LINE

Sometimes enough is enough. You have to draw the line. Then, "having done all to stand," as the Scriptures say, "stand" (Ephesians 6:13). Even if standing means taking a black eye or a bloody nose. Remember back when we were kids at recess or at the ballpark and some big kid was bullying everyone? Finally, a brave kid stepped up and called the bully out. Heated words were exchanged. Threats were made. "Who's gonna stop me?" asked the ever confident bully.

"I am," the brave kid responded.

"Alright. Make me."

The showdown was on. The brave kid drew a line in the dirt with his foot or a stick, and crossing his arms he declared through gritted teeth, "You better not cross this line or else..."

There are times in life when something rises up in us and we have to draw a line to make a stand against or for something. As adults we draw different kinds of lines that are far more significant than those on the playground. We've all heard people say things like, "You can mess with me, but if you mess with my family, that's the line you don't cross!" When it comes to the killing of America and saving our freedoms, we have to ask ourselves, "Where do we draw the line? When is enough, enough?"

There are other times lines are drawn as a challenge, calling us to join others stepping out and over the line into the battle. The phrase "drawing a line in the sand" has its origin all the way back to 1836 and the Alamo. During the Texas Revolution, Texas was fighting to win independence from the evil Mexican dictator General Antonio Lopez de Santa Anna, after which it would be invited to become the 28th state of United States.

Today, if you visit the Alamo there's a statue honoring a Texas Hero, Lt. Colonel William Barret Travis. The plaque reads: "Legend states that in 1836, Lt. Col. Willian Barrett Travis unsheathed his sword and *drew a line on the ground* before his battle-weary men stating, 'Those prepared to give their lives in Freedom's cause, come over to me!'"

All but one or two of the Texas heroes joined Travis on the other side of the dirt line. They understood that freedom for their families and nation would come at a cost they were willing to pay. Whatever happened to them individually was worth it. Those are difficult words to swallow, but throughout history that's what it often took for change to happen. Though Mexico ultimately won the Alamo battle, 189 Texan defenders took out an estimated 1,600 of the enemy. It cost the Texans their lives, but it so depleted the Mexican army that it allowed the ultimate war to be won.

Just weeks later, the Texans would win their independence at the Battle of San Jacinto. What happened at the Alamo became a rallying cry. Texan General Sam Houston reportedly motivated his troops at San Jacinto with the words, "Remember the Alamo!"

Whether drawing a line to take a stand against evil or stepping over a line into the battle, either way, drawing the line is all about freedom.

THERE'S ALWAYS A RISK AND A COST

Throughout the Bible, God's faithful have drawn lines to take stands or step up into action. When they did, there was always a risk and a cost to pay. Yet God always showed up in different ways that impacted change. Let's briefly look at a few to remember like Sam Houston's troops remembered the Alamo!

Who can forget the three Hebrew young men, Shadrach, Meshach, and Abednego, who served in Babylonian King Nebuchadnezzar II's court. Forget those Sunday school flannel board depictions. These guys were in their prime, probably 16 to 21 years old. Highly respected, they were the best-looking, the most intelligent, and carried out duties in the palace and were set over the affairs. Daniel 1 says they were:

> *...Israelites from the royal family and the nobility—young men without any physical defect, handsome, showing aptitude for every kind of learning, well informed, quick to understand, and qualified to serve in the king's palace. ...God gave knowledge and*

> *understanding of all kinds of literature and learning. ...In every matter of wisdom and understanding about which the king questioned them, he found them ten times better than all the magicians and enchanters in his whole kingdom* (Daniel 1:3-4, 17, 20 NIV).

In other words, these guys were the cream of the crop who lived like and were treated like royalty. The one catch was, they served the one true God and knew to whom they belonged, and it wasn't King Nebuchadnezzar II. It's important to note that consistently throughout biblical history, God placed His servants smack in the middle of the world's kingdoms, at key positions.

Despite all the accolades and royal comforts, there was a line the three Hebrews would not cross even if it meant losing their status and well-being, even their lives. There was a lot to lose if they took a stand, and staying safe would be easy. Just bow down. That's all. Nope. That was the line. They would die instead of bowing.

The king didn't cheer their courage, like the culture today won't cheer ours. Refusing to bow royally hacked the king off and you know the rest of the story. Ol' King Neb heated up the fiery furnace seven times hotter than usual and tossed the three men in while fully clothed in their robes and sandals and turbans. You can imagine just how hot that was if you've ever opened the Thanksgiving turkey oven and felt like your eyebrows and eyelashes just melted off!

The king was making a statement. Most scholars believe the "fiery furnace" was likely some sort of humongous fire pit. Regardless, it was hotter than hot, but the three Hebrews didn't burn. Instead, a fourth man "like the Son of God" (Daniel 3:25 NKJV) showed up in the fire with them.

He'll show up in the midst of our fires too. That's what God does and He's going to do in America when we start drawing lines.

Nebuchadnezzar was so shaken up that he decreed, "that the people of any nation or language who say anything against the God of Shadrach, Meshach and Abednego be cut into pieces and their houses be turned into piles of rubble, for no other god can save in this way" (Daniel 3:29 NIV). Then the king promoted the three godly men in the province of Babylon. I'd say their stand impacted the nation and created a tidal wave of change right in the wicked pit of Babylon.

Let's talk about Daniel. He was the mentor of those three young Hebrew men. Eventually, however, King Darius of Persia seized Babylon and executed Nebuchadnezzar III. Yet because of Daniel's ability, Darius befriended him. On top of his game, Daniel had influence, favor and power within the hierarchy of the government. His future was bright.

> *Now Daniel so distinguished himself among the administrators and the satraps by his exceptional qualities that the king planned to set him over the whole kingdom* (Daniel 6:3 NIV).

You see that? Daniel's future was set. He was going to be overseer of the whole kingdom. However, because he was a child of the one true God and had principles, there was a line he wouldn't cross. And the day came when Daniel had to draw that line and he knew the cost and the risk.

Basically, Daniel's enemies wanted him out but couldn't find anything corrupt about him. Because they knew Daniel would be faithful to his God, they tricked Darius into writing and ratifying a law that proclaimed for 30 days no one could pray to anyone else but King Darius, otherwise they would be thrown in the lion's den. The crooked politicians published the decree throughout the kingdom, knowing Darius would have to honor it after the people saw it.

Does this sound familiar? We're not mentioning names, but we seem to have some corrupt politicians who will stop at nothing to destroy certain men[1] and women who stand[2] against the killing of America.[3] Like with Shadrach, Meshach, and Abednego, all Daniel had to do was not pray for 30 days. Just do nothing. That's it. He could have prayed silently, in private, and no one would have ever known. Instead, because of principle, Daniel drew a line and prayed three times a day facing Jerusalem with his windows open so everyone could hear. He was making a bold statement.

How many Christians fall into the "do nothing" category? Perhaps elections would have swung in a different direction if they just did something, like vote, or threw their windows open and spoke up, making their voices heard, even if ridiculed or canceled. Daniel knew the risks. Loss of livelihood, honor and life—the lion's den. Like the three Hebrews were tossed into the fire, Daniel was tossed into the hungry lions' den. This time, instead of the fourth man showing up in the fire, God sent an angel to muzzle the mouths of the lions.

In the morning, Darius was so beside himself with joy, he proclaimed, "I issue a decree that in every part of my kingdom people must fear and reverence the God of Daniel" (Daniel 6:26 NIV). And Daniel prospered. He was another tsunami of light that overpowered the attempted tsunami of darkness, because one person drew a line and stood their ground.

THE FIRST DOORDASH EMPLOYEE

Finally, consider David. Forget the flannel board depictions. It began pretty much like every other mundane day. David, 16 to 19 years old, working in the fields as a shepherd, was given a simple assignment to deliver lunch and supplies to his older brothers' camp where they were out doing battle. He was the first DoorDash employee. For those who may not be aware, DoorDash is an online delivery company that is taking the nation by storm. You select your food from a variety of restaurants, enter your address, and voila, someone drops it off at your door.

David's dad said, "Hey, take this lunch to your brothers." David was just delivering lunch. I bet he didn't even get a tip for door-dashing.

His brothers were "mighty" warriors in Israel's army. Their job was to protect God's chosen people. They were also David's heroes, warriors he longed to be like one day. So when he had the opportunity to go where the action was, he leapt. Yet when David arrived, he found his warriors anything but "mighty." And he was appalled. Israel's great protectors, his brothers included, were all cowering in fear while the enemy giant Philistine and their army taunted them.

Goliath was mocking God and His people. Instead of manning up, Israel's warriors "fled from him and were dreadfully afraid" (1 Samuel 17:24 NKJV). While they retreated in fear, godly indignation rose up inside David. "Are you kidding me?" David must have thought. Maybe that's where David J. Harris Jr. got his famous "Are you kidding me?" line. Maybe he got that line from the original David. "How could you possibly think about food at a time like this? Forget lunch!" David couldn't take seeing his God and culture being defiled. "No! Not on my watch. Ain't gonna happen. I'm drawing a line!"

Historians tell us that possibly in an effort to minimize bloodshed, the Philistines had been issuing a challenge to the Israelite troops of one-on-one combat—their best warrior-dude, Goliath, against Israel's best warrior-dude. It was winner-take-all and a common practice in ancient warfare. The challenge had been going on for 40 days. The Philistines were relentlessly attacking God's people and imposing on their land. The problem was no one on Israel's side had stepped up.

Eventually, after convincing Saul to let him, David stood before Goliath. When he showed up as an unconventional, pretty-boy lunch deliverer with no armor and no spear, Goliath didn't take him seriously.

Is there something holding you back from doing what God has told you to do? Is age your hang-up? Physical or financial limitations? God delights in using the most unexpected people for extraordinary victories. He then gets all the credit. So you're not getting off the hook and you have no excuses that are good enough for not getting involved and doing what God's been talking to you about doing in this war.

"What do you mean, talking to me about?" Well, have you ever gotten "a good idea" that was really outside your realm of a "good idea" on your own? We're here to tell you that wasn't (most likely) your good idea, but it's what we call a "God idea."

Often, we mistake them for "our ideas" and want to get credit for them. If it's an idea out of the blue and something you normally wouldn't have thought of on your own, it's most likely a "God idea." God most likely dropped it off. Now if you want to claim it as your own (pride), you might not get any more of those really wonderful ideas. But if you thank God for it and acknowledge that it came from Him, we're here to tell you those "God ideas" are going to keep on coming.

> *And when the Philistine looked about and saw David, he disdained him; for he was only a youth, ruddy and good-looking. So the Philistine said to David, "Am I a dog, that you come to me with sticks?" And the Philistine cursed David by his gods. And the Philistine said to David, "Come to me, and I will give your flesh to the birds of the air and the beasts of the field!"* (1 Samuel 17:42-44 NKJV)

The threats and intimidation didn't faze David one little bit. A line had been drawn. He had to stand up for truth and righteousness. Instead of allowing himself to be paralyzed by fear like the others, David ran toward Goliath full-out, with full confidence, slinging that stone as he ran! Failure was never an option. In David's mind it was a done deal. The giant was going down. And he did! A perfect shot, David slung the stone, but the Holy Spirit directed it right between the giant's eyes sending him to the dirt with a loud thud.

David didn't have a sword of his own, so he took the giant's and cut off his head. It wasn't a pretty scene. David wasn't being nice. You know exactly what I'm talking about. We want to play it safe and not offend anyone or ruffle too many feathers. David didn't care who he offended as long as it wasn't his God.

Here's the really cool part. When Goliath went down, watch what happened: "…And when the Philistines saw that their champion was dead, they fled. Now the men of Israel and Judah arose and shouted, and pursued the Philistines…. Then the children of Israel returned from chasing the Philistines, and they plundered their tents" (1 Samuel 17:51,53 NKJV). When they saw David's courage and that the giant fell, they rallied and chased down the rest of the enemy. Drawing lines and stepping up causes others to follow. Maybe you're being called to draw a line, step up, and be a leader right now?

Time doesn't permit us to write in-depth about Esther, who put her life on the line for her people. There was a line drawn challenging her to step across into the battle that would cost her something. When Mordecai learned of the plot against the

Jewish people and shared it with Esther, he challenged her with these famous words:

> *Do not think that because you are in the king's house you alone of all the Jews will escape. For if you remain silent at this time, relief and deliverance for the Jews will arise from another place, but you and your father's family will perish. And who knows but that you have come to your royal position for such a time as this?* (Esther 4:13-14 NIV)

After hearing Mordecai's words, Esther drew a line. Her response was, "I will go to the king, even though it is against the law. And if I perish, I perish" (Esther 4:16 NIV). Being killed was a very real possibility. King Ahasuerus had executed or banished his queen Vashti before Esther for not flaunting her beautiful body at a party. That's how wicked this culture of power was. Even so, Esther didn't remain silent; she stepped up for her people. God gave her favor with the king, and he listened to her plea. Because of Esther's willingness to step up at that exact moment in time and do what she needed to do, even if it meant death, God used her to save a nation.

Notice, every hero or heroine we've mentioned had to get to the line in the sand, willing to "risk it all." We should all be willing to risk it all for our God-given freedoms, truth and righteousness. It's time we let some holy indignation rise up in us. You have to ask yourself, "Who am I taking lunch to?" Watch for opportunities to confront the giant. It may be your moment to step up and defend our nation. You have been placed where you are for such a time as this.

WE KEEP MOVING THE LINE

Sometimes, though, we're like David's warrior brothers and don't step up and across to battle; or instead of standing firm on the lines we've drawn, we step back and draw new lines.

"Or you'll what?" The bully on the playground snapped back, unflinching, while he took a huge step of defiance right over the line. Instead of standing firm, the brave kid who drew the line trembled and took a step backward. He's losing his nerve. Then, he gets a little courage and draws another line in the dirt. The bully laughs and steps right over it again, this time giving the boy a shove. The boy stumbles back, gets a little courage again, and draws another line. The bully snickers and does the same thing again. This process repeats itself with the bully gaining more confidence and territory each time.

Finally, the bully says, "Whatever," and leaves his timid opponent to resume terrorizing the playground. He won. He figures all talk and no action. The kid goes back to shooting hoops, saddened, but relieved for the moment because the bully has left. He's comfortable for now, just not free. The kid knows what the bully is doing to the other kids, and that he'll be back.

This same scenario has played out in America over and over. Why do we keep backing up, giving territory, and drawing new lines? You give the devil an inch, he'll take a foot. You give the devil a foot, he'll take yard. You give the devil a yard, he'll take a mile. Then it's your block, then it's your city, after that your country.

A friend of mine who is a New York Times bestselling author was in a grocery store shopping when a 90-year-old woman grabbed him by the arm and shook him urgently. Mila was her name, and she knew who he was. "The same things I saw back then, shortly before the fall, I see happening now! We must stop it! We must."

Mila and her parents and their families went through the revolution in St. Petersburg, Russia, under Vladimir Lenin's Marxist and communist rule. Truly horrifying things were commonplace, like her grandmother waiting in line for a whole day to get food handed to her in a brown paper package inside of which were two ox hooves. That was food. They would cook rotten potatoes in rancid grease, just trying to find anything to eat.

And there was a constant fear because her grandmother had been arrested. Her father was arrested, and her grandfather's two brothers were arrested. And the grandfather and the two brothers were executed and buried in a mass grave somewhere, as was one of their wives who was seven months pregnant. It was brutal. She remembered seeing a countess wrapped in rags in the snow begging because she had nothing. Everything had been taken from her, including her dignity. The progression is usually from socialism to Marxism to communism.

Mila and her parents escaped Russia through various harrowing ways and settled in Riga, Latvia. Soon, however, it became clear that Russia was about to take over Latvia. And so, her father begged America through the embassy to take them. Finally, America came through and allowed her and her parents to come, leaving relatives behind. One grandmother starved to death, and the other was hauled off to Siberia, never to be heard from again. Thank God for America.

Still, they had to enter legally. In order to come to America, a family had to sponsor them. Mila's parents sent out letters to people all across the United States asking for a sponsor. Finally, a precious minister in Virginia responded and said, "Come here. We have a place for you." They took the minister up on his offer, and the church housed them in their church fellowship hall until Mila's father found work and they could get on their feet.

It's an incredible story of the giving heart of the American people and how at that time, America understood how critical protecting our borders is and how serious the path to citizenship should be. It's a privilege and an honor to become a citizen of this country that should not be taken lightly.

It's important to point out that when Mila shook my friend's arm in the grocery store saying, "The same things I saw back then shortly before the fall, I see happening now! We must stop it! We must!" While those things were happening in Russia, her family was living a quite comfortable, wealthy life. They were a family of professionals. Her father was a physician and the head of a hospital in St. Petersburg until the revolution. And then it was gone.

Today, our modern society thinks it could never happen here, but it is happening right before our eyes. The technology and methods are different, but the ideologies trying to kill America are the same. If we don't act, at some point there will be an overnight takeover similar to the Covid lockdowns. Knowing this, we keep moving the lines of resistance back. Why?

Fear.

We can be paralyzed by fear.

FEAR

In the last chapter, we wrote that there was a tangible presence of fear in Russia. The Soviet government knew if they could keep the people in a state of paralyzing fear they could be controlled. It worked. But how did the people get to that point? Little by little, beat down after beat down, they kept moving the line back, allowing the godless agenda to gain emotional and physical territory.

We call it "the shock collar effect." When training a dog to stay in a certain area where you don't want a visible fence, you install an underground electric fence and put a shock collar on your dog. Every time the dog attempts to cross—bam, the dog feels a shock. This happens again and again and again. Over time, the dog's will to run free is broken and it doesn't even go close to the fence. In many cases, once the dog is trained, the shock collar can be removed because it will never challenge the fence again.

This is in essence what is happening to us. Every time we attempt to cross their lines, we get shocked. And it hurts. We're labeled "racists," "haters," "homophobic," "transphobic," "terrorists," on and on. We are punished unjustly by the two-tiered justice system.[4] January 6 protestors have been imprisoned,[5] vilified,[6] lost their incomes,[7] while left-wing protestors burn down whole sections of cities,[8] crush cars, beat up innocent citizens, shoplift, and loot with zero consequence.[9] They cancel us, humiliate us, fire us, and arrest us. Shock. Shock. Shock.

While writing this, an Austin, Texas, elementary teacher was fired by administrators who said they were concerned about her "intentional attempt in teaching students about their legal and constitutional rights."[10] Shock.

In 2023, a seventh-grade honor student at a Massachusetts middle school was punished and sent home for wearing a "there are only two genders" t-shirt.[11] He wasn't disturbing anyone or attacking any other beliefs, but that didn't stop his school from censoring him. Shock.

During Covid, thousands of workers across America were fired for refusing to get the jab. Shock.[12]

You know the "shocking" stories.[13] We could fill a library. People are living in fear, afraid to speak up or stand up. Just keep your mouth shut and let them have their way. Think about if you're in DC right now, you walk into the Capitol, and a police officer says, "Hey, come on in." You might think twice about entering, wouldn't you? How did we get here? Shock. Shock. That's how.

A TODDLER'S TENACITY

Fortunately, some of us are born "slap happy" and "shock proof" and even were prepared for the consequences with a smile on our face. Before the invention of protective plug covers, we know of a toddler who absolutely loved to stick his finger into the wall socket. The mother would say sternly, "No!" A smile from the toddler, and right there in front of Mom, he would shove the finger back into the socket. Escalating, he went from "No!" and a mild slap on the hand, progressing to more smiles and successive attempts at the wall socket and eventually a beet-red hand. We're guessing that's why those safety covers were made.

We have to get focused like that toddler (on a positive goal, mind you) and determine to keep at it, not allowing the shock or the slap to deter us from our goals, and have a smile on our face as we go.

We would love to paint some nice, clean scenario, but this is a nasty reality. These are Goliaths threatening to take our voices away. Unless we start drawing lines and refuse to back up or start crossing the lines that are calling us to step up and over into action, America is done. Some giants have to fall, or America is dead.

Hear what we are not saying. We are not advocating for violence. America is not at that point.

Fortunately, we still have avenues available to us to stand up for change, but we have to act and be prepared for the consequences. We have to get comfortable with being uncomfortable. Thankfully, America is not dead yet.

I can't think of a better place to share this incredible piece of writing titled "The Valor and Bravery of the Unvaccinated," written by French General Christian Blanchon:

> Even if I were fully vaccinated, I would admire the unvaccinated for standing up to the greatest pressure I have ever seen, including from spouses, parents, children, friends, colleagues and doctors.
>
> People who have been capable of such personality, courage, and such critical ability undoubtedly embody the best of humanity. They are found everywhere, in all ages, levels of education, countries and opinions. They are of a particular kind; these are the soldiers that any army of light wishes to have in its ranks. They are the parents that every child wishes to have and the children that every parent dreams of having. They are beings above the average of their societies; they are the essence of the peoples who have built all cultures and conquered horizons. They are there, by your side, they seem normal, but they are superheroes.
>
> They did what others could not do; they were the tree that withstood the hurricane of insults, discrimination and social exclusion. And they did it because they thought they were alone and believed they were alone. Excluded from their families' Christmas tables, they have never seen anything so cruel. They lost their jobs, let their careers sink, and had no more money...but they didn't care.

> They suffered immeasurable discrimination, denunciations, betrayals and humiliations...but they continued.
>
> Never before in humanity has there been such a casting; we now know who the resisters are on planet Earth. Women, men, old, young, rich, poor, of all races and all religions, the unvaccinated, the chosen ones of the invisible ark, the only ones who managed to resist when everything fell apart. Collapsed.
>
> You've passed an unimaginable test that many of the toughest marines, commandos, green berets, astronauts and geniuses couldn't pass. You are made of the stuff of the greatest that ever lived, those heroes born among ordinary men who shine in the dark.[14]

A TIME TO PREACH AND A TIME FOR ACTION

In the basement of the U.S. Capitol, there's a statue of a man named Peter Muhlenberg. Most are not aware of who he was. Peter's father, Henry Muhlenberg, was responsible for the Lutheran Church being established in the United States, and Peter was a Lutheran pastor as well.

The reason his statue is in the Capitol is because of his famous action that happened on January 21, 1776. After he gave his famous sermon based on Ecclesiastes 3:1 (ESV), "For everything there is a season, and a time for every matter under heaven," he closed his message with the words, "In the language of the Holy Writ, there is a time for all things. There is a time to preach and a time to fight. And now is the time to fight."[15] At that point, Pastor Peter Muhlenberg threw off his clerical robes to reveal the uniform of an officer in the Continental Army. Drums began to roll, men kissed their wives, and they walked down the aisle to enlist. He walked out and that day 300 men connected with him, and they went to go fight for the American Revolution. Here's a guy who was a pastor who drew a line and stood up.

Peter was in Woodstock, Virginia, while his brother Frederick Muhlenberg, also a minister, was in New York. Frederick responded like a lot of pastors do now. He was like, "Oh, Peter, you're kind of overreacting. We need to preach and stay in the church. We're not supposed to cross the line. We're not supposed to be in politics. We're supposed to be preachers."

And Frederick continued that way until 1794 when the British burned down his church. When they did that, suddenly Frederick decided he was going to join the fight. These are the people our nation is founded upon. Frederick joined the military, then later ended up serving as Secretary of State and Speaker of the House. Peter Muhlenberg was a general in the Revolutionary War and ended up serving as senator and several key appointments in our government. But what's interesting is that they were two pastors. It was highly unusual to step out of that position—and to wear a soldier's uniform under your priestly robes was unheard of.

Peter Muhlenberg was so important to America that there's a statue in the basement of the Capitol. There is a statue of him in a park in DC as well. And it's one of those statues you walk by and go, "I wonder who that is?" This is the guy who was the founder of the Black-Robed Regiment. And so, everybody points back to that pastor.

That's the essence of what we are doing through this book and *Flashpoint Live*. We're motivating individuals, ministers, business leaders and teachers to get out of their robes of complacency and go stand up for what's right. Again, this is not a call to violence, but to fight through the constitutional means available to us by making our voices heard.

Peter's own brother didn't agree with him until they burned down his church. And what was the outcome of his brother getting involved? He fought the fight in the American Revolution. Which is kind of what's going on with America now. Unfortunately, it seems like most people are like his brother. They don't get involved until it comes into their backyard. The "What you do in your bedroom is your business" attitude has gotten us where we are today.

We have to understand our role as believers and as patriots who love and believe in America. There has to be a line that you won't let someone cross, whatever the risks and costs. But the truth is we can draw some lines that will make a real difference that aren't all that risky. They are just uncomfortable.

We can't be woke Christians in our Nike shoes that we bought at Target, sipping our Starbucks latte while we plan our vacation to Disney and expect change. We are feasting at tables we should be flipping over. Has the church gone woke? Where is the line you won't cross?

David confronting Goliath was only his beginning. He had to run from Saul for years! He had to fight for the promise God gave him.

Do you have skin in the game? Will your beliefs cost you anything? God is saying to every one of us: How far will you go? Will you stand up for Christ? Will you tell an unforgiving, spiteful world that Jesus loves them while they call you homophobic and Christo-fascist? Will you still give to a ministry when it's not tax deductible anymore?

We ask you—will it take a loved one dying from getting the Covid vaccine or dying in the hospital from their drug-induced big pharma protocol (like happened to one of our family members) before you get involved? Will it take your child getting ripped from you, genitals mutilated and/or in hormone therapy (like happened to one of our family members), before you'll get involved? How about someone you love dying from fentanyl? A known illegal, convicted criminal murdering someone you love before you decide to draw the line in the sand? Does it take a child or a grandchild to be sexually abused and/or trafficked?

Let's all be wiser and quicker to respond to the bully and the line in the sand than Frederick Augustus Muhlenberg was. We implore you, be a Peter Muhlenberg versus a Frederick. Do not wait till personal tragedy comes raging at your door before you decide you might need to get involved.

NOTES

1. Darren Samuelsohn, et al., "Roger Stone arrested in Mueller investigation," *Politico,* January 25, 2019; https://www.politico.com/story/2019/01/25/roger-stone-arrested-following-mueller-indictment-1125445; accessed April 20, 2024.
2. Joshua Nevett, "Trump's legal battles: How six cases may play out," *BBC News,* November 15, 2020; https://www.bbc.com/news/world-us-canada-54716550; accessed April 20, 2024.
3. Grace Dean, "Mike Lindell's lawyers said Dominion and Smartmatic's 'conspiracy' against him is set to cost the MyPillow CEO more than $2 billion," *Business Insider,* June 4, 2021; https://www.businessinsider.com/mike-lindell-dominion-smartmatic-donald-trump-biden-voter-fraud-lawsuit-2021-6?op=1; accessed April 20, 2024.
4. Richard A. Epstein and Tom Church, "Law For Thee, But Not For Me," *Hoover Institution;* https://www.hoover.org/research/law-thee-not-me-thoughts-two-tiered-justice-system; accessed April 20, 2024.
5. Aleks Phillips, "Full List of Capitol Rioters Jailed So Far and the Sentences They Are Serving," *Newsweek,* September 12, 2023; https://www.newsweek.com/full-list-capitol-rioters-jailed-sentences-january-6-1826075; and Alexander Mallin, "Capitol rioter to serve 8 months in prison in 1st felony sentencing from Jan. 6, ABC News, July 19, 2021; https://abcnews.go.com/US/capitol-rioter-serve-months-prison-1st-felony-sentencing/story?id=78925742; both accessed April 20, 2024.
6. Gabrielle Fonrouge, "Capitol rioter dies by suicide because of 'broken heart' over case"; *New York Post,* March 2, 2022; https://nypost.com/2022/03/01/

jan-6-capitol-rioter-dies-by-suicide-because-of-broken-heart-over-case/; accessed April 20, 2024.

7. "Mike Lindell's lawyers…," *Business Insider,* June 4, 2021; https://www.businessinsider.com/mike-lindell-dominion-smartmatic-donald-trump-biden-voter-fraud-lawsuit-2021-6?op=1; accessed April 20, 2024.

8. Nina Moini, "After last year's unrest, some businesses rebuilt. But many have not recovered," *MPR News,* May 26, 2021; https://www.mprnews.org/story/2021/05/26/after-last-years-unrest-some-businesses-rebuilt-but-many-have-not-recovered; accessed April 20, 2024.

9. Jeff Dunetz, "Thieves Going Wild in California, Taking Advantage Of State Law Protecting Shoplifters," *The Lid,* September 28, 2019; https://lidblog.com/california-shoplifters/; accessed April 20, 2024.

10. Paige Hubbard, "AISD teacher termination stirs up controversy," *CBS Austin,* June 8, 2023; https://cbsaustin.com/news/local/cbs-austin-exclusive-aisd-teacher-termination-stirs-up-controversy; accessed April 20, 2024.

11. Snejana Farberov, "Student claims he was sent home over shirt that said "there are only two genders'; *New York Post,* May 1, 2023; https://nypost.com/2023/05/01/boy-says-he-was-sent-home-over-shirt-that-said-there-are-only-two-genders/; accessed April 20, 2024.

12. Anne Knox Averitt, et al., "Get Poked or Get Canned—Can You Terminate an Employee for Refusing the Vaccine?" *The National Law Review;* September 23, 2021; https://www.natlawreview.com/article/get-poked-or-get-canned-can-you-terminate-employee-refusing-vaccine; accessed April 20, 2024.

13. Andrea Hsu, "Thousands of workers are opting to get fired, rather than take the vaccine," *NPR,* October 24, 2021; https://www.npr.org/2021/10/24/1047947268/covid-vaccine-workers-quitting-getting-fired-mandates; accessed April 20, 2024.

14. Christian Blanchon, "The Valor and Bravery of the Unvaccinated," *VeteransToday.com,* September 9, 2022,; https://veteranstoday.com/2022/09/09/french-general-pays-tribute-to-the-antivax-they-seem-normal-but-they-are-superheroes/; accessed April 20, 2024.

15. Peter Muhlenberg, quoted in "American Minute with Bill Federer," October 2, 2023; https://americanminute.com/blogs/todays-american-minute/john-peter-muhlenberg-major-general-congressman-senator-pastor-with-his-pastor-brother-frederick-first-speaker-of-u-s-house-american-minute-with-bill-federer; accessed April 20, 2024.

5

RIGHTS AND REWARDS

On April 30, 1789, at daybreak, hundreds of people began gathering outside the Federal Hall in New York City. They came to witness the inauguration of George Washington as the first president of the United States. Before the throng of witnesses, Washington placed his hand on an open Bible and pledged his oath to God and America. Then, he reached down and kissed the Bible. Upon doing so, the crowd burst into cheers. That alone is enough to give our opponents, (those who want God out and to kill America), fits.

It gets better.

After being sworn in, Washington made his way to the Senate chamber where he gave his inaugural address before a joint session of Congress. In that speech he said:

> Not without resorting once more to the *benign* [caring] *Parent of the Human Race* [God] in *humble supplication* [prayer] that, since He [God] has been pleased to favor the American people with opportunities for deliberating in perfect tranquility,

> and dispositions for deciding with unparalleled unanimity on a form of government for the security of their union and the advancement of their happiness, so His [God's] *divine blessing* may be equally conspicuous [obvious].[1]

Though a bit difficult to read, those words are nothing less than staggering and incredibly significant to our cause. Basically, George Washington was saying that through prayer and humble dependence upon the creator God, his divine favor on America will be obviously clear. Following Washington's address, the inaugural party proceeded to St. Paul's Chapel, where the Episcopal Bishop of New York led a divine service of celebration. "Te Deum," an early Christian hymn of praise, was the lead-off song. The hymn's opening Latin words, *Te Deum laudamus*, are translated as, "Thee, O God, we praise."

The inaugural party had a worship service! They were praising God for the blessing of America and for our first president who was clearly a man of faith. Don't ever let anyone try to convince you that America was not founded on biblical principles by believers with a solid Judeo-Christian worldview. It's simply not true.

Since that first inaugural ceremony, the Bible has been used in the inauguration of all the presidents except three. "In God we trust" is on our currency for a reason. As "One nation under God" is in our Pledge of Allegiance. Granted, they were added later, but with the full approval (votes) from Congress. Groups have since pushed to have the phrase removed, yet the Supreme Court continues to uphold the right for those words to remain.

God and the Bible are common threads woven throughout America's history. In remarks at a prayer breakfast in Dallas, Texas, in August 1984, President Ronald Reagan said, "If we ever forget we are one nation under God we will be one nation going under."[2] Still, those intent on killing America are revisionists who want to erase our godly history and reinvent it without God or the Bible.[3] But their history is a lie, and their radical agenda won't work. History, real history, has shown time and again that it is a recipe for a corrupt and unhinged society.

We must draw the line and take a stand and not move the line back regardless the costs. If you take God and His governing principles out, you ultimately end up with the tyrannical state we're seeing increase.

When God's morality is rejected, it is replaced by man-made philosophies based on whatever their particular bent is at the time. Because there are no absolutes in their minds, the standards of right and wrong become fluid. Fluid seems to be a new term that keeps popping up these days. Fluid, in its most practical sense, means there is no fixed standard and can easily flow from one form to another. A fluid can be liquid or gas. This is the principle they want to apply to gender and everything else in culture. No fixed standard.

The archenemy of fluidity is absolutes. Forget what common sense or biology says; because if there is no God, nothing is absolute. Therefore, as they are trying to reinvent history to fit their warped ideas, they are also attempting to reinvent reality to justify their sinful lunacy. Everything is fluid; therefore, everyone does what's right in their own eyes.

The problem is man's nature is inherently corrupt. The Bible says that in Israel when they had no king, "everyone did what was right in his own eyes" (Judges 17:6 ESV). Concerning this, Matthew Henry wrote, "Every man did that which was right in his own eyes, and then they soon did that which was evil in the sight of the Lord."[4] The lines between good and evil had been erased.

When a society gets to that point, it's a slippery slope. Evil is tolerated, then accepted, then demanded, and finally celebrated. Tyranny ultimately takes hold, and suffering becomes the norm for the masses. It's progressive. Beating people up on the streets becomes okay. Vandalizing private property is justified. Shoplifting and looting is a right.[5] Parents voicing their concerns are labeled terrorists.[6] Doing mutilating, life-changing, trans-gender surgery on minors and providing affirming health "care" behind their parents' backs is considered ethical.[7]

In our opinion it reminds us of an Alice-in-Wonderland utopia (an imagined place where everything is perfect) no matter what the rules. Drag queens performing for elementary children is applauded. On and on it goes. If there is not a change, lawlessness and depravity will continue to explode. But again, in a brilliantly inspired way our founding fathers foresaw this and prepared.

Notice that in his inaugural address, George Washington referred to the "divine blessing." He understood that if America followed godly principles, she would experience the evident favor of God.

There is a way to get it back.

RIGHTS

If we are going to save America, we must move forward with the full authority that is rightfully ours. Half speed won't cut it. When David sprinted toward Goliath, he wasn't being all polite and nice. No. He was talking smack, throwing it right back in the big guy's face. "Today the Lord will conquer you, and I will kill you and cut off your head; and then I will give the dead bodies of your men to the birds and wild animals, and the whole world will know that there is a God in Israel!" (1 Samuel 17:46 TLB). That's some serious smack! There was no timidity there. David knew his rights. He knew his God. We need to start getting a little holy smack in us, but in order to do that, it's vital that we understand this next point and then own it.

Whenever our founding fathers talked about the separation of church and state, it was never intended to eliminate God and restrict people of faith from being involved in government. No matter how loud the opposition yells, "Separation of church and state!" to intimidate us into silence, like Goliath shouted his insults and threats to intimidate Israel, the truth is the exact opposite.

Separation of church and state simply means that there can be no state-enforced religion or church. In other words, the government cannot tell you where or how to worship. You are free to worship in whatever form you want. You are free and to be treated equally, even if you are an atheist or believe something contrary to my beliefs. The government cannot coerce people to believe or conform to a particular religious practice. No official state church. That is not what saving America is about.

We are not trying to make America one big church. No. The church is and always will be separate. However, separation of church and state does not mean that people of faith cannot or should not be involved in or influence government by their faith. The truth is the founding fathers wanted us to be involved in and influence government with our faith. The separation of church and state was to restrict the government, not it's people!

But our opponents hate that right and hate us. Our response should be like David's to Goliath, "I don't care what venomous lies you are spewing. I know my God and I know my rights. You can't silence me!"

When George Washington leaned down and kissed the Bible, he wasn't worried about offending the unbelievers in the crowd. Undoubtedly, there were some. That's okay. We have the right to offend, and people have the right to not accept what we are saying. That is America.

Founding father Thomas Paine remarked, "He who dares not offend cannot be honest." We have a lot of dishonest people running around because they are afraid to speak their minds. Have you noticed, everybody seems to be offended these days and nobody can do or say anything because they are afraid to offend? They are afraid, not so much of what people think of them, but the cultural punishment.

Not so with David, and it shouldn't be with us. The Gospel itself is an offense to many, but it's truth. They will hate us and want to shut us up. "Whoever would overthrow the liberty of a nation," said George Washington, "must begin by subduing the free acts of speech."

Killing America starts with killing God and then killing our free speech.

Case in point. In June 2023, Governor Sarah Huckabee Sanders of Arkansas was criticized and reprimanded by the liberal left because her children created Christian chalk artwork on the driveway of the governor's mansion. The liberal reasoning was simple: "How dare you hold public office and allow your children to promote Christianity on public property. It violates the Establishment Clause. Someone might be offended. We're offended."

But the governor knew her rights and responded to the demands to remove the drawings saying, "...my answer is, 'No.' I will not erase the beautiful cross my kids drew in chalk on the driveway of the Governor's Mansion or remove my post on social media, and I will not now or ever hide that I am a Christian."

She further shared that she believes it is a misinterpretation to claim the U.S. Constitution "prevents government officials, let alone their families, from making earnest expressions of religious faith." Governor Huckabee Sanders went on to say, "You are asking me to ignore that truth and hide a crucial part of my identity and the identity of my kids. ...That I will not do." She concluded her response by saying people of any faith are welcome at the governor's mansion.[8]

In the minds of those who oppose us, you can't be in public office and actually live your faith out loud. That is unacceptable and goes against their questionable lifestyle. You must celebrate them or resign and be quiet.

But their protest is based on a lie. We have every right to influence, even if it offends some. We can't let them intimidate us into silence. We are not saying don't be compassionate and loving. We have to be a light of hope to a dark world, but sometimes loving is flipping tables. After all, Jesus did make a whip of cords (see John 2:15). Have you ever thought about that? Not very timid.

What those killing America are really saying is, "We can bring our godless philosophy into your government, but you can't bring your God or faith into our government." They want you to embrace their sin and have our government, which is our tax dollars, pay for their sinful lifestyles. Of course, we absolutely do not have the right to violate another person's individual rights unless it is doing harm to someone else, but we certainly have the right to bring our faith and its impact into our culture via the voting booth and legislative branches. We still have that right.

Encouraging and electing people of faith into the legislative branches of government, particularly on the local levels, is vital. That means you can get involved. And what happens on the local and state levels ultimately affects the national levels. It can start a ripple, and then a wave, and even a tsunami.

We are already seeing it. Some very positive things have happened as a result of our voices and votes that we still have. I mean, who would have thought Roe v. Wade would have been overturned and sent back to the states where locals have a voice? That is an incredible victory. Recently, the Supreme Court has given conservatives some major victories.

> Joe Kennedy, an assistant high school football coach in Washington state, has accepted a $1,775,000 settlement package from the school district that fired him over his post-game prayer ritual after a court found the move unconstitutional.[9]
>
> In a Fourth of July Landmark ruling a Federal District Court ordered the government to immediately end their mass-censorship operation targeting Americans who talk about election fraud, Covid, vaccines and other important issues. This is a *huge win* for the First Amendment and a *huge loss* for government officials who work in elections, public health, and other agencies. We the People will *not* be silenced.[10]

As we wrote this very chapter, a report in *The Christian Post* was headlined, "Pride messaging down 40% from 2022 as boycotts explode." The article went on to point out that:

> Shoppers everywhere have made punching bags out of Bud Light and Target, [Nike, Kohl's, and Disney]—forcing several of American brands to reconsider just how much capital they're willing to sacrifice. As the losses to those brands dip into the multi-billions, there's a growing sense that businesses are getting the message. ...That's a seismic shift for the U.S. market and an enormous victory for grassroots Americans who've finally put their dollars where their values are. ...When a good 40% of your consumer base ups and walks away, there

> should be plenty of motivation for corporations to sit down and rethink their politics.[11]

Nothing speaks louder than the pocketbook. Be encouraged! We are not powerless! We still have rights, and we have rewards. However, we must continue to exercise and fight for our rights, or we *will* surely lose them. Yes, they are vocal. They are loud. We don't need to try and outshout them. We need to sprint full-out toward the enemy's face with absolute confidence, knowing our rights. Not in arrogance, but with humble dependence on God, as our first president so elegantly encouraged.

We think there is a correlation between the malicious attacks at those exercising their First Amendment rights that don't line up with the approved narrative(s). Those they attack most viciously are those they fear the most. The more they attack innocent people[12] and let criminals go unpunished or lightly punished,[13] the more we Americans are wising up and pushing back. We need to remember the quote "one for all and all for one" from *The Three Musketeers.* We are all in this together, and whenever they unjustly go after one, they will do it to you if you do not get involved. Once again, remember, "We the people."

If you are reading this book and feel a stirring inside you to save America, then you are called for such a time as this. Focusing on your own circle of influence, whether small or large, will help create a tsunami of light and change. As the article pointed out, "That's a seismic shift." Well, seismic shifts are what cause tsunamis! We are not backing down. We've got a big job to do and we have to get going.

Speaking on the powerful impact the boycotts[14] are having on woke corporations, Dr. Ben Carson said:

> And the only people who can change that is we the people. …We have to put our foot down and say, this is America. This is where we are free to live the way that we want to, to worship the way we want to, to say what we want to say. And we're not going to stand for government or corporate America to try to dictate [what we think and believe].[15]

REWARDS

We have to know our rights, but we also have to know and claim our rewards. Yes, David stepped up and confronted Goliath for a noble cause, but he also knew there was a big reward being offered of Saul's daughter and a life free of taxes. He wanted that reward and wasn't ashamed to claim it. David never considered how many had possibly tried and died before he showed up. He wasn't considering the cowards hiding behind the boulders and trees. He was thinking, "This is what I get if I knock off that giant. I'm getting that reward." We have to think, "What is our reward when our giant goes down? What and who are we fighting for? What will America look like when we win?"

Another important fact to note here is that at this point, David had already been anointed the future king. He knew that his reward at some point was to be crowned as the king of Israel.

Yet after he killed Goliath, David served Saul until Saul became jealous and tried to kill him. Then, David was on the run for another 17 years before he saw the fulfillment of his reward. We have to have that same kind of resolve and trust. Even though David had rights and the reward coming, he had to fight for it.

It's about perspective—seeing the other side and knowing your reward that is coming. Why did David have to live on the run? Because he had been censored. He was canceled because of his popularity among the people. "Saul has killed his thousands" they danced and sang, "David has killed his ten thousands" (1 Samuel 18:7 NCB).

While on the run, David and his men lived in hiding inside caves and in the wilderness. David was used to that. One time he acted like he was a crazy man in the middle of the field so they would walk right by him. This does not sound victorious. This is not in the victory manual of how you're supposed to look when you are pursuing and waiting for your reward.

DUTY IS OURS; RESULTS ARE GOD'S

Even though the founding fathers intended the United States of America to be a nation without slavery, this didn't happen right away. In the beginning years of our nation's history, the majority of Congress was opposed to the emancipation of slaves. Despite this fact, one man fought tirelessly for the freedom of America's slaves. This man was John Quincy Adams. For 28 consecutive years, he consistently fought for this cause—even when it seemed that he was making no progress at all.

One day, while he was leaving the Capitol building, a reporter stopped him and asked why he kept pushing for the emancipation of slaves when it seemed hopeless. Adams turned, looked at the reporter, and said simply, "Duty is ours; results are God's." He then walked on.

In 1847, a man who looked up to Adams came to serve in Congress as a freshman legislator. Soon, Adams took this man under his wing and became his mentor—they grew so close that this man was a pallbearer at Adams's funeral. After one term in the legislature this man went home, and Adams later died after serving 28 years in the legislature—seeing none of the fruits of his labor.

Now some time after Adams's protégé returned home, he ran again for office, and again, and again. In fact, he lost multiple elections, but one of the elections he did win was the most important one—the race for the seat of the President of the United States. This man's name was Abraham Lincoln. He went on to be one the most important presidents in our nation's history—and the one who ended up freeing America's slaves.

John Quincy Adams's response to the reporter's question was an extremely wise one. He understood that you cannot be distracted by what you see when working toward a goal; you have to live by faith and trust that God will bring out the fruits of your labor.

While we are leading the change, we must always remember to keep our eyes on the goal up ahead like Adams did. We must always remember that "Duty is ours, results are God's." The Lord knows what He is doing, and He knows when the day will come when Americans will once again recognize God's hand in the affairs of men.[16]

We've had a misaligned, misconstrued idea of what victory looks like. We know what it sounds like, but we don't always know what it looks like. We think we're going to stand up and Disney is going to fold just like that. Nothing would make us happier than for Disney to change or sell out immediately to some Christian company whose leadership promotes biblical values. But most of the time, change takes time, sometimes a long time.

We have to take this to the next place. We have to know our reward is out there for us to claim, yet we must be patient, persistent, and permanent. If you tap on a piece of brick wall long enough, eventually it will crack and then break, but you have to keep tapping.

NOTES

1. "President George Washington's First Inaugural Speech (1789)," *National Archives,* https://www.archives.gov/milestone-documents/president-george-washingtons-first-inaugural-speech; accessed April 20, 2024.
2. President Ronald Reagan, "Remarks at an Ecumenical Prayer Breakfast in Dallas, Texas," August 23, 1984; *Ronald Reagan Presidential Library & Museum*; accessed April 21, 2024.

3. CRC Staff, "Generational Worldview Shift: Millennials Seek World without God, Bible, Churches," Arizona Christian University, May 14, 2021; https://www.arizonachristian.edu/2021/05/14/generational-worldview-shift-millennials-seek-world-without-god-bible-churches/; accessed April 20, 2024.

4. Matthew Henry, *Concise Commentary on the Whole Bible*, Judges 17:6; https://biblehub.com/commentaries/judges/17-6.htm; accessed April 20, 2024.

5. "Bill to Stop Employees Confronting Shoplifters Passed by California Senate," *Newsweek,* June 6, 2023; https://www.newsweek.com/store-retail-violence-robbery-theft-stealing-california-1804565; accessed April 20, 2024.

6. Robby Soave, "A.G. Merrick Garland Tells FBI To Investigate Parents Who Yell at School Officials About Critical Race Theory, *Reason.com,* October 6, 2021; https://reason.com/2021/10/06/ag-merrick-garland-fbi-critical-race-theory-parents-schools-domestic-terrorists/; and "US House Judiciary Republications: DOJ labeled dozens of parents as terrorist threats," *Judiciary Committee* press release, May 20, 2022; https://judiciary.house.gov/media/press-releases/us-house-judiciary-republicans-doj-labeled-dozens-of-parents-as-terrorist; and Maud Maron, "Why Are Moms Like Me Being Called Domestic Terrorists?" *The Free Press,* October 11, 2021; https://www.thefp.com/p/why-are-moms-like-me-being-called; all accessed April 20, 2024.

7. Lindsey Tanner, "Trans kids' treatment can start younger, new guidelines say," *Los Angeles Times,* June 16, 2022; https://www.latimes.com/science/story/2022-06-16/trans-kids-treatment-can-start-younger-new-guidelines-say ; accessed April 20, 2024.

8. Billy Hallowell, "Sarah Huckabee Sanders' Resolute Response to Demands She Remove Kids' Cross Chalk Drawing," *FaithWire,*

July 3, 2023; https://www.faithwire.com/2023/07/03/i-will-not-ever-hide-that-i-am-a-christian-sarah-huckabee-sanders-resolute-response-to-demands-she-remove-kids-cross-chalk-drawing/; accessed April 20, 2024.

9. Ari Blaff, "Praying Football Coach Receives Nearly $2 Million Settlement from School District," *National Review,* March 20, 2023; https://www.nationalreview.com/news/praying-football-coach-receives-nearly-2-million-settlement-from-school-district; accessed April 20, 2024.

10. Kari Lake, social media post, July 4, 2023, https://gettr.com/post/p2l9tiob112.

11. Suzanne Bowdey, "Pride messaging down 40% from 2022 as boycotts explode," *The Christian Post,* July 6, 2023, https://www.christianpost.com/voices/pride-messaging-down-40-from-2022-as-boycotts-explode.html; accessed April 20, 2024.

12. Sharon Basch, "US dispatch: recent SCOTUS rulings contribute to a divided Fourth of July," *Jurist.org,* July 4, 2023; https://www.jurist.org/news/2023/07/us-dispatch-recent-scotus-rulings-contribute-to-a-divided-fourth-of-july/; accessed April 20, 2024.

13. Elizabeth Stauffer, "Grandmother, 69, with Cancer Reports to Prison for Jan. 6 Charges, Has Message for Americans," *The Western Journal,* July 15, 2022; https://www.westernjournal.com/video-grandmother-69-cancer-reports-prison-jan-6-charges-message-americans/; accessed April 20, 2024.

14. Jon Seidel, et al., "A gun charge filed during George Floyd rioting in Chicago is dismissed amid controversy," *Chicago Sun Times,* March 29, 2024; https://chicago.suntimes.com/the-watchdogs/2024/03/29/

bruen-supreme-court-operation-legend-heriberto-carbajal-flores-george-floyd; accessed April 20, 2024.

15. "Disney Faces Renewed Boycott Calls," *Newsweek,* November 30, 2023; https://www.newsweek.com/disney-renewed-boycott-calls-elon-musk-1848243; accessed April 20, 2024.

16. Savannah Barry, "Duty is ours, results are God's," *Patriot Academy,* https://www.patriotacademy.com/duty-is-ours-results-are-gods/; accessed April 20, 2024.

6

WEAPONIZE YOUR WOUNDS

Abraham Lincoln has been credited with the saying, "You can fool some of the people all the time, all of the people some of the time, but you cannot fool all of the people all of the time." The far-left, woke progressives think they are fooling us, that they can deceive us and keep us controlled while advancing their killing of America.

There's a lot packed into that sentence. You might want to reread it and let it soak in. As the dear Russian lady Mila in the supermarket urged to my writer friend, we can't let history repeat itself.

Mila explained in the beginning she lived in prosperity, comfort, and freedom. Then, slowly, bit by bit, things changed. Like a frog in warm water that slowly heats up to a boil. The frog never jumps out. By the time it realizes what is happening, it is too late.

Mila said it got to the point that no one could debate politics or the government. If you disagreed, you were called evil. Then you were labeled so you could be dehumanized. After you were labeled, the government that once protected them, was weaponized against the "labeled" ones.[1] House arrests began in a method of controlling and monitoring of their every move.[2]

Soon, they cut off the people's ability to work. That enabled control of food and health care. It got to the point where they were starving. Whoever rose up in desperation and refused compliance were shipped to a prison camp or killed.

All of this was unthinkable in the beginning. This could never happen to them. This dear woman, Mila, was emphatic about getting the word out and stressing that we must never let this happen again. She thought they were immune. She was deeply concerned she was seeing similar things happening in America now.

The same tools that the Nazis used to dehumanize the Jews, are same kind of tools that are being deployed in today's America.[3] We would highly recommend that you watch Eric Metaxas's documentary, "Letter to the American Church" on EpochTV.[4] Eric Metaxas does an excellent job of explaining what happened during that time period.

We who love America and want to bring it back to greatness are often viewed as just uninformed, backward, gun-totin', Bible-thumping conspiracy theorists who are a cancer on society. Have you ever talked to a far-lefter? Let's just say, humility is not one of their stronger traits. In fact, instead of engaging in fruitful debate, most resort to insults and laughing because they see themselves as superior in intellect.

Instead of talking to us, they talk above us so they can dismiss us. This is also one of the core characteristics of the mainstream media. They see themselves as so far above the regular "Joes" like us. But it is the regular people who are the heartbeat of this nation and keep the lifeblood flowing through it.

In our opinion, elitists bombarded us with lies and false information about Covid cures and lockdowns and masks and vaccines and Russian collusion and racism—among a host of other lies. They shut down our businesses and churches, while allowing other businesses and bars to remain open. It was illegal to gather at church but not Home Depot. All of it was an attempt to control us.

Sure, they fooled some of us for some of the time, but never all of us all of the time. There were those voices crying in the wilderness, warning us, pointing out the lies and hypocrisy, even the solid science. But those voices were ridiculed and canceled. Not anymore. The truth came out and they're no longer fooling us. Their tactics aren't working. All they are doing is poking a wounded bear. And that's not a very smart thing to do! They are overplaying their hand and underestimating us. We know our rights and aren't afraid to use them. That's why they are scrambling to conceal or outright change our "inalienable" rights.

In our opinion, elitists actually believe the average conservative American can't think for themselves. Oh, we can think, alright. We actually do follow the science and common sense. We can recognize the truth from a lie, no matter how many times the lie is repeated. We can look at someone and know for certain from the clear biology if they are male or female.

We understand, unlike some in our government and universities, that just because someone identifies as something doesn't make it so. We see the absolute ridiculousness when Time Magazine puts a man dressed up like a woman on their cover and calls him the "Woman of the Year."[5] We personally cannot celebrate unbiblical ideologies. We, of course, as Christians love the LGBTQIA+ people, but to not tell the truth about the consequences of that lifestyle has eternal negative repercussions for them.

We know that men are not able to have babies. If a transgender identifying as a man has a baby, it is in reality a woman having a baby. Dylan Mulvaney,[6] the infamous Bud Light transgender, is a man identifying as a woman and came out as a lesbian. In other words, he's a man who likes women! There is something deep inside us that craves the truth.

Yes, conservatives are grounded in reality. We are perfectly capable of absorbing the facts, actual facts, and making sound, educated, reasonable assessments. We don't need a woke régime making decisions for us or for our children. It doesn't take a village to raise healthy children, only loving parents whose authority isn't being undermined. Yet that is exactly what they are doing. Of course, they know much more than us and can make better decisions than us, for us. The educators are much more "educated" and informed than the parents. Well, mama bear and papa bear have been wounded and poked!

During the Second World War, Nazi Germany encouraged and trained their young children to spy on their parents and turn them in. Stalin and Mao did the same thing. It was an effort to undermine and destroy family unity and trust in order to build an army of youth to recreate a Nazi or communist society.

Why do we repeat this disturbing and sobering fact from history? We do not want history to repeat itself! What is going on today in our public schools and universities is eerily similar. Parents who don't toe the LGBTQIA+ woke agenda line and don't embrace Critical Race Theory—along with a host of other ungodly, hate-America propaganda that's being force-fed down their children's throats—may be labeled as terrorist extremists.[7]

Yet, we feel the reality is that the actual terrorism is the wokeism being executed against our children and their parents. A concerned and brave retired educator confronted her own local school board with the following words:

> There is no way a young boy or girl voluntarily will go into a school counselor's office to say he or she wants a gender change *unless* in the classroom, and in special school clubs, and is done in secret without parents' knowledge, they are groomed and brainwashed to do so. They are hostile to the nuclear family and want to abolish it by turning the children against their parents. Now, who is the Nazi? The parents who love and support their children, or the school systems, the educators, the woke socialist?[8]

What we understand is this—for the left, education is all about conversion. There is another documentary that we feel is a must-see for anyone who has children in their life whom they love. It is a YouTube video, titled "Art Club."[9]

We have on a personal level, experienced the same thing in an accelerated public school in Texas. They are more interested in converting our children than teaching the fundamentals needed to succeed in life like reading, math, real science, English, and accurate history. As a result of this nonsense, America is falling woefully behind. "U.S. Education Rankings Are Falling Behind the Rest of the World." The U.S. placed eleventh out of other countries in science, and "the top five math-scoring countries were all in Asia."[10]

So many of "we the people" believe that this is due to some of our leaders being bribed by other countries who want to be world dictators and destroy our sovereignty. We believe woke educators are more concerned about not offending a non-binary student by using a biological pronoun than engaging them in the actual science.

Not long ago, there was a song and video performed by gay activists that went viral on social media. The words should send chills down the spines of concerned parents, grandparents, and those who want to save America:

> As we celebrate pride and the progress made we've these past years, there's still work to be done.
>
> ...You think that we'll corrupt your kids if our agenda goes unchecked. Funny, just this once you're correct. We'll convert your children. Happens bit by bit, quietly and subtly, and you will barely notice it. ...We don't care. We'll convert your children.

> We'll make them tolerant and fair. …But I see now why you'd have a problem with that. Just like you worried, they'll change their group of friends, you won't approve of where they go at night to protest, but when you'll be disgusted when they start finding things online that you've kept far from their sight—like information. …We're coming for your children. …Will work to convert all their sisters and brothers.[11]

Wake. Up.

America.

Of course, proponents of the video maintain it's simply satire and not to take it seriously and those who do are portraying "typical ignorant behavior." There you go, it seems if you criticize or show any concern, you are ignorant and hateful. Yet the undeniable facts that are playing out are anything but satire. We don't want to sound fatalistic—but yes, they are absolutely coming for our children.[12]

There's a quote, purportedly by Edmund Burke, that we've heard countless times, but it's never been truer than today. It goes, "The only thing necessary for the triumph of evil is for good men to do nothing."[13] Well, papa and mama bear are rising and are on the defensive! They have been awakened out of hibernation.

WHY IS WOKEISM SO SIGNIFICANT TO THE KILLING OF AMERICA?

Before we go any further, we need to answer the question: Why is wokeism so significant to the killing of America? Why not just let people live their lives as they please and we live our lives the way we please? What's the big deal? The big deal is not so much for you not to have the freedom to do what you want. We want you to have the freedom to do what you want with your life, even for you to make poor and even sinful choices. That's your right. We believe in free will and free choice.

The problem is when anti-biblical behavior is being forced on us and our children to agree with and embrace and participate in. The forces that be are weaponizing their agendas against free America. They want to control us down the line and wokeism[14] is a tool that allows them to do that.

Do you think the government actually cares if a man thinks he's a woman or vice versa? They couldn't care less. They see it as a way to garner votes and political power. It's the same thing with Covid lockdowns and mandates, open borders, even AI—artificial intelligence. All of it is being weaponized against us. This is why it's so vital to stop it. We're not trying to limit people's freedom. We're trying to ensure everyone's freedoms, because ultimately even the LGBTQ2+ wind up being victims of this ungodly agenda. In the end, if things keep going like they are, everyone loses.

Let's take the issue of debt for a moment. You may be thinking, "What in the world does debt have to do with LGBTQ2+ and weaponizing these issues?" More and more, we are working on a cashless, electronic basis. Transactions are usually done on a card or cellphone. If you are financing with the bank, your mortgage and vehicles and all your transactions are being handled electronically.

Ultimately, the government wants to bring us to a point where if we fail to meet their standards, whatever they dictate, they can cut you off, restricting access to your funds until compliance.[15] They can control your spending, travel, and even take your home or land because you can't pay. They control us when they have access to all our funds electronically.[16]

This is already happening in China. China has the most advanced, massive surveillance system in the world, and their citizens function almost 100 percent on a cashless, electronic basis. Whenever someone breaks a rule, whatever it is, they get points deducted from their card— punishing them by limiting their purchasing ability.

Currently, the Chinese government has installed more than 200 million surveillance cameras across their country, which amounts to approximately one camera per seven citizens.[17] China's social credit system ranks citizens and punishes them with throttled internet speeds, flight bans, [and limiting purchasing ability] if the Communist Party deems them untrustworthy.[18] So literally you have citizens living as prisoners under the electronic system. We saw Canadian Prime Minster Trudeau do the very same things to truckers when they protested.[19] He froze their finances. It's what communism looks like.[20]

Those killing America want to bring that system to America. They are already implementing it. They want to get to the point where if you fail to do what they say—whether it's misgendering someone, failing to comply with one of their lockdown mandates, posting something on social media that they determine as "hate speech,"[21] whatever they deem unfit—they can cut off your finances, take your home and land, starve you.

This is not an exaggeration, and if the good people of this country do nothing, we're going to wake up one morning to the shock of our lives. Some people already are. If at all possible, get out of debt.

Another reason the spiritual enemy behind the scenes is pushing the wokeism agenda along with open borders allowing fentanyl[22] and criminals[23] to come in[24] and now AI (artificial intelligence), is to depopulate the world.[25] Add to those agendas the fact that satan has successfully used the courts and medical system to abort approximately 60 million babies since 1973. Just think if those babies were alive today—the taxes they would pay, the contributions, potential inventions and leadership, the love missed out on, all sorts of good things that never happened because the enemy snuffed out their lives.

Evangelist Marilyn Hickey said that God had told her when she was praying about a cure for AIDS that one had been sent. But the person with the cure had been aborted. When people are gay or trans, they don't reproduce.[26] They may adopt,[27] but they don't reproduce.[28] Think of that. The more that ideology progresses, the less the population reproduces. Little by little, bit by bit, like they say, it will reduce the conservative Judeo-Christian voices. The enemy's goal is a world without God.

NO GRANDCHILDREN TO CUDDLE

True story. There's a couple who are friends of ours who definitely want grandchildren.

They have two sons who are incredibly charismatic, handsome, charming, and gay. This couple's boys were incredibly popular in the public school system, but then they got groomed. Being gay or "bi" or trans is now considered interesting and cool,[29] whereas being straight is boring[30] and being a Christian is worse.[31]

Brought up in a solid church with a very godly youth pastor, the oldest son came out as gay first. He was leery because he had been taught it was wrong. It is wrong. He struggled with his choice. His school educators rallied around him, supporting him, encouraging him to come out. Once he announced he was gay, he became so popular in school it was like an addictive drug. He was even voted the class president and Mr. Senior. Pushing his struggles aside, he dove headlong into the lifestyle.

Soon after, his younger brother followed in his older brother's footsteps, wanting to be just like his hero. The parents, godly people who love the Lord, were beside themselves not knowing what to do. They sought counseling from their pastor and Christian counselors. The dad, a man's man, had his heart ripped to shreds. The mom spiraled into deep depression. Meanwhile, the two sons were surrounded with gay friends and a gay school support system that encouraged them that their parents were "sweet" people, but just didn't understand reality. The parents eventually found other like parents within the Christian community as a support group. They decided in God's grace to love their boys even though they disagreed with them.

The two sons are now grown and have been through multiple relationships, something common in the gay community. Both sons moved to New York City and then to Orlando to work on a Disney cruise ship. There were no weddings with beautiful brides. No daughters-in-law. And no grandkids, no one to carry on the family name.

Though these parents love their sons and they are moving on with life, there is a sadness and loud quietness around their home. This is an all too common scenario across America. To the average person this story may seem out of the realm of normal, but the sad reality is these kind of stories are becoming the norm. We're seeing it every day with families across the nation.

Add to our dilemma the fentanyl that is pouring across the border, killing hundreds of thousands of youth every year. In 2022, 110,000 died from fentanyl.[32] Already, by July 2023, that number is being surpassed.[33] China produces fentanyl and funnels it to cartels in South America and Mexico to smuggle into America.[34] The cartels want to make money. Other countries appear to want to kill America.

We have to ask ourselves why the government wants to lock us down to prevent the spread of Covid[35] but refuses to lock down the border to prevent the tsunami of fentanyl and criminals who hate[36] America. Makes you scratch your head and go, "Hmm." To put it in perspective, more Americans have died of fentanyl deaths in the last decade than in World War I, World War II, the Korean War, and the Vietnam War combined.[37]

America is at war. Yet if you want to close the borders you are a racist, bigot, ignorant, uncompassionate hater. Why?

Meanwhile, artificial intelligence is threatening with some scary stuff. Radical AI is another attempt by the enemy to eradicate humans.[38] We know that some who will read this will shuck it off as just another over-the-top conspiracy theory, but again, the facts are stacking up just as did with the vaccine. Some of us were labeled as conspiracy nuts when we questioned "the jab." The truth is now coming out as thousands suffer from vaccine injuries and sudden death.[39]

We're seeing, as mentioned earlier in the book, that those labeled as "conspiracy nuts" weren't so dumb after all and were actually courageous.

Back to the AI situation. With the rampant shoplifting, looting, and violent crime sweeping America, also encouraged by the far left, more stores, particularly in blue states (state that predominantly vote for or support the Democrat Party), are turning to AI. They can't afford to lose merchandise and pay employees to run them, so they are turning to robots and machines.

The following are a few headlines for you to consider. "First McDonalds with No Human Employees Opens in Fort Worth, Texas."[40] The article begins with, "I've seen robots serving coffee and flipping burgers in sci-fi movies, but what if we told you that you can experience that in real life?"[41]

Here's another headline, "Amazon is rolling out AI across a dozen of its largest warehouses." And another, "Automated Trucking—Autonomous Driving Trucks.[42] How AI is disrupting the trucking sector."[43] Forbes Magazine published an article titled "The 15 Biggest Risks of Artificial Intelligence."[44] The article points out that:

> AI technologies often collect and analyze large amounts of personal data, raising issues related to data privacy and security. ...The risk of AI development being dominated by a small number of large corporations and governments. ...AI-driven automation has the potential to lead to job losses across various industries, particularly for low-skilled workers. ...AI-generated content, such as deepfakes, contributes to the spread of false information and the manipulation of public opinion. ...The development of artificial general intelligence (AGI) that surpasses human intelligence raises long-term concerns for humanity.[45]

This is *Forbes Magazine,* not some conspiracy publication. Of course, *Forbes* pointed out that there are positives to AI technology that we should embrace, but the positives are not the problems. It's the evil in society that always seems to find a way to manipulate for more power and control. Perhaps our founding fathers could see into the future; that's why we must cling to our constitutional rights.

Yes, this is real life, not conspiracy. Just as the woke mob is coming for your kids and grandkids,[46] AI is wanting to restructure society as we know it.

Yes, we can "experience" the wonders and benefits of artificial intelligence, but there is always a dark side—always.[47] It will be weaponized against us. When you put it all together—wokeism, the border crisis, election integrity, electronic funds, and artificial intelligence—it makes for an Orwellian society.

This following story is essential before we move on. We have to tell you because these things we've been sharing are so close to home and we want to shake you up with how real all this really is.

There's another couple close to us who had a then-16-year-old daughter who was raised in a wonderful church. Beautiful and intelligent, she tested in the gifted and talented category. This being the case, her parents thought it would be a good thing to put her in a special accelerated high school for gifted students where she would be challenged and could get an advanced degree with college-level courses.

This cutting-edge school was difficult to get into and the parents trusted the educators with their daughter. Now, we must say here that there are many wonderful, godly teachers in the public school system. Thank God for them. They are on the front lines, and we need more.

Everything was peachy until the parents began noticing small, incremental changes in their daughter's behavior and personality. Then, when she suddenly chopped off her beautiful hair, they knew something was up and did some investigating. What they uncovered was the shock of their lives. To start with, Mom started digging through her daughter's iPad and cellphone late at night. This is a perfectly suitable action for parents of a 16-year-old living at home.

It was discovered that the daughter was going to numerous LGBTQIA+ websites. Then they found out that their beautiful daughter had sent a letter to the school telling them her preferred pronouns. She wanted to go by "him." A friend had helped her construct the letter. Then if that wasn't enough, on her iPad was a video she had recorded of a group of adults telling kids how to come out to their parents. They were laughing about it, obviously cooler and more understanding than their unsupportive, unenlightened parents who didn't agree with their choice.

A line was drawn in the sand when they discovered that one of their daughter's teachers and counselor was openly transgender, and that several of the teachers were LGBTQIA+. They had been grooming their daughter, encouraging her to question her sexuality and gender identity and to enroll in gay and trans clubs. It even went so far that the school was providing a dressing room so she and others like her could come from home and change into her transgender clothes, which included a breast binder. You can't make this stuff up. The so-called support groups at school turned the daughter against her parents if they didn't support her.

When the parents found out about all this, they were devastated. Mom became like that wounded mama bear, and everybody knows you don't mess with a wounded mama bear. At least if you know what's good for you!

A plan was devised, and she checked her daughter out of school one day for a mom/daughter lunch date. After lunch, mom didn't take her back to school. Instead, they pulled her out permanently and had a Christian school prepared to take her. They had contacted the Christian school and were working with them because their daughter had to agree to go there for school .

The whole ordeal was like detoxing an addict off of drugs. She screamed and hollered and there was drama and refusing to talk. It took a while before she would even go visit the Christian school. Meanwhile, they received a call from her former school, saying, "You need to come in and pick up her stuff and drop off her books and sign some paperwork."

When Mom arrived at the school, however, it was a setup. They wanted her to wait for the principal. She could feel the judgmental arrogance directed her way and that they were going to barrage and bully her. But Mom was prepared, and when they found out that there could be a serious lawsuit, the school suddenly backed off.

This is a very real scenario that is still playing out with their daughter. It's a long road to healing and wholeness. Thank God for parents willing to draw the line and step up to rescue their daughter who didn't know she needed rescuing. Bears are most dangerous when they are wounded, and they're even more dangerous when their babies are wounded.

WEAPONIZE YOUR WOUNDS

We said all that to say that Christians need to get outside the church walls and affect change in the community and culture through tough love. Just like mainstream media weaponizes their agendas against us, Christians must weaponize our wounds to get America and our kids back. When you've got skin in the game and you have wounds, there's pain and there are tears and there is weeping.

In First Samuel 30, before David was king, when he along with his mighty men were on the run from Saul, for a period of time they lived with their families in a village called Ziklag. At one point David and his men went away for about three days to do whatever warriors do. In this particular season, David was self-confident and failed to seek God's guidance. As a result, when the men left for their little outing, they carelessly left the village unguarded. When we fail to seek God, we often leave important things unguarded.

After their trip, upon arriving back home to Ziklag, instead of being greeted by warm kisses and hugs from their wives and children, they found the village completely devastated. The aroma of cooking filling the air was replaced with the smell of charred, burning structures. Worse, the Amalekites who raided their village had taken off with their valuables, including their most prized treasures—the wives and children.

> *And when David and his men came to the city, they found it burned with fire, and their wives and sons and daughters taken captive* (1 Samuel 30:3 ESV).

The next verse says, "So David and his men wept aloud until they had no strength left to weep" (1 Samuel 30:4 NIV). These mighty warriors, men with armor and swords, wept until they had no more strength to weep. Have you ever been there? You weep until there is no more energy in your body. You wail and cry out and tears become your words. This is where these guys were. They were weeping for their sons and daughters. They were weeping for their wives and families. They were weeping that their community was invaded and destroyed. They were weeping about their failure to protect their treasures. To say they were wounded would be an understatement.

But watch what happens.

After a period of arguing among themselves and blame shifting, David becomes so heavy-hearted that he pours himself out to the Lord.

> *David was greatly distressed because the men were talking of stoning him; each one was bitter in spirit because of his sons and daughters. But David found strength in the Lord his God* (1 Samuel 30:6 NIV).

As David finds strength "in the Lord his God" and is renewed, he questions God about what to do next. "So David inquired of the Lord, saying, 'Shall I pursue this troop? Shall I overtake them?'" (1 Samuel 30:8 NKJV). Look at God's response: "Pursue, for you shall surely overtake them and without fail recover all" (1 Samuel 30:8 NKJV).

With the Lord's help, David rallied his 600 men and took off pursuing the enemy. They weaponized their wounds and moved with fierce passion.

> *So, David recovered all that the Amalekites had carried away, and David rescued his two wives. And*

> *nothing of theirs was lacking, either small or great, sons or daughters, spoil or anything which they had taken from them; David recovered all* (1 Samuel 30:18-19 NKJV).

They recovered everything the enemy had stolen plus some!

Just as the enemy raided Ziklag, he has raided our families and communities. In so many ways a lot of us are devastated. America's sons and daughters have been taken captive by vain philosophies—relativism, secularism, hedonism, marxism, satanism, etc.—and woke brainwashing. We've been wounded, but our time of weeping is over. It is time to pursue, overtake and recover all. To do that we're going to have to get bold.

So we're praying for you that a Holy Spirit boldness come on to you like you've never had before. From our own personal experiences, many of our institutions, including educational systems, are turning out an army of trans kids and are openly recruiting, and they are looking for kids who are hurting.

Time is of the essence. There is a whole generation of kids the enemy has tried to rip away from the kingdom of God. He's trying to destroy them because they are made in the image of God. He doesn't want them reproducing and wants to mock them in front of God.

Spiritually, we must stand in the gap for revival in the next generation because they are the next Jesus Movement. The enemy is trying to pervert and ultimately destroy the apple of God's eye—His kids made in His image.

In our perspective, many of us have been wounded. We do have skin in the game. We must weaponize our wounds and let God empower us to make bold choices that impact change. Are we willing to pursue and recover what has been stolen? What is going on is serious. It's life and death. It's imprisonment and slavery by stealing our children's innocence through sexual perversion and destructive ideology such as CRT.

They are burning America to the ground.

NOTES

1. Summer Lane, "Bombshell Undercover Investigation Goes Viral for Exposing Dirty CIA 'Entrapment,'" *RSBN,* April 9, 2024; https://www.rsbnetwork.com/news/bombshell-undercover-investigation-goes-viral-for-exposing-dirty-cia-entrapment/; accessed April 21, 2024.
2. M. Dowling, "FBI Agents Visit a Woman Over Her Social Media Posts," *Independent Sentinel,* March 29, 2024; https://www.independentsentinel.com/fbi-agents-visit-a-woman-over-her-social-media-posts/; accessed April 21, 2024.
3. "How Nazi propaganda dehumanized Jews to facilitate the holocaust," *elpais.com,* December 4, 2022; https://english.elpais.com/society/2022-12-04/how-nazi-propaganda-dehumanized-jews-to-facilitate-the-holocaust.html; accessed April 21, 2024.
4. Eric Metaxas, "Letter to the American Church," documentary, *EpochTimes,* February 8, 2024; https://www.theepochtimes.com/epochtv/letter-to-the-american-church-5569329; accessed April 21, 2024.

5. "Dylan Mulvaney Wins Woman of the Year Award," *Newsweek,* October 12, 2023; https://www./newsweek.com/Dylan-mulvaney-wins-woman-year-award-18343571; accessed April 21, 2024.

6. Jay Valle, "Bud Light partnership with trans influencer Dylan Mulvaney prompts right-wing backlash," *NBC News,* April 5, 2023; https://www.nbcnews.com/nbc-out/ou-pop-culture/buud-light-partnership-trans-influencer-dylan-mulvaney-prompts-rightwin-rcna78295; accessed April 21, 2024.

7. John Malcolm, "Are Parents Being Tagged as 'Domestic Terrorists' by the FBI? Justice Department Needs to Show Its Cards," *The Heritage Foundation,* November 18, 2021; https://www.heritage.org/crime-and-justice/commentary/are-parents-being-tagged-domestic-terrorists-the-fbi-justice; accessed April 21, 2024.

8. Retired school teacher confronts the school board; https://www.tiktok.com/@lexitmovement1/video/7237218316622859563.

9. The Art Club, transgender indoctrination, *YouTube,* November 17, 2023; https://www.youtube.com/watch?v=EgKGiXmgqZs; accessed April 21, 2024.

10. Kimberly Amadeo, "U.S. Education Rankings Are Falling Behind the Rest of the World," *The Balance,* March 26, 2023; https://www.thebalancemoney.com/ the-u-s-is-losing-its-competitive-advantage-3306225; accessed April 21, 2024.

11. San Francisco Gay Men's Chorus, "A Message from the Gay Community," *YouTube,* July 9, 2021; https://www.youtube.com/watch?v=ArOQF4kadHA; accessed April 21, 2024.

12. "They Are Coming For Your Children," *Family Policy Alliance,* June 27, 2023; https://familypolicyalliance.com/

issues/2023/06/27/they-are-coming-for-your-children/; accessed April 21, 2024.

13. "The Only Thing Necessary for the Triumph of Evil is that Good Men Do Nothing"; https://quoteinvestigator.com/2010/12/04/good-men-do/?amp=1; accessed April 21, 2024.
14. Michael Karson, PhD, JD, "The Psychology of 'Wokeism,'" *Psychology Today,* August 9, 2021; https://www.psychologytoday.com/us/blog/feeling-our-way/202108/the-psychology-wokeism; and "U.S. Office of Personnel Management: Guidance Regarding Gender Identity and Inclusion in the Federal Workplace," https://www.opm.gov/policy-data-oversight/diversity-equity-inclusion-and-accessibility/reference-materials/guidance-regarding-gender-identity-and-inclusion-in-the-federal-workplace.pdf; both accessed April 21, 2024.
15. Kristin Tate, "Coming soon: America's own social credit system," *The Hill,* August 3, 2021; https://thehill.com/opinion/finance/565860-coming-soon-americas-own-social-credit-system/; accessed April 21, 2024.
16. "Are Financial Institutions Using ESG Social Credit Scores to Coerce Individuals, Small Businesses?" *The Heartland Institute,* February 27, 2022; https://heartland.org/publications/financial-institutions-are-expanding-esg-social-credit-scores-to-target-individuals-small-businesses/; accessed April 21, 2024.
17. Alexandra Ma, "China is building a vast civilian surveillance network—here are 10 ways it could be feeding its creepy 'social credit system,'" *Business Insider,* April 29, 2018; https://www.businessinsider.com/how-china-is-watching-its-citizens-in-a-modern-surveillance-state-2018-4; accessed April 21, 2024.
18. Bernard Marr, "Chinese Social Credit Score: Utopian Big Data Bliss Or Black Mirror On Steroids?" *Forbes,* January 21, 2019;

https://www.forbes.com/sites/bernardmarr/2019/01/21/chinese-social-credit-score-utopian-big-data-bliss-or-black-mirror-on-steroids/?sh=4646ecc948b8; accessed April 21, 2024.

19. Brian Platt and Jen Skerritt, "Banks freeze millions in convoy funds under Trudeau edict," BNN Bloomberg, February 22, 2022; https://www.bnnbloomberg.ca/convoy-leader-denied-bail-as-canadian-officials-warn-of-unrest-1.1727032; accessed April 21, 2024.
20. "Communism," *National Geographic;* https://education.nationalgeographic.org/resource/communism/; accessed April 21, 2024.
21. "Hate speech," *Britannica,* April 13, 2024; https://www.britannica.com/topic/hate-speech; accessed April 21, 2024.
22. Steven Reinberg, "U.S. Deaths Due to Fentanyl Nearly Quadrupled in 5 Years," *U.S. News and World Report,* May 3, 2023; https://www.usnews.com/news/health-news/articles/2023-05-03/u-s-deaths-due-to-fentanyl-nearly-quadrupled-in-5-years; accessed April 21, 2024.
23. "Criminal Noncitizen Statistics," *U.S. Customs and Border Protection,* April 12, 2024; https://www.cbp.gov/newsroom/stats/cbp-enforcement-statistics/criminal-noncitizen-statistics; accessed April 21, 2024.
24. "Border Rescues and Mortality Data," *U.S. Customs and Border Protection,* March 29, 2024; https://www.cbp.gov/newsroom/stats/border-rescues-and-mortality-data; accessed April 21, 2024.
25. Cade Metz, "What Exactly Are the Dangers Posed by A.I.?" *The New York Times,* May 1, 2023. https://www.nytimes.com/2023/05/01/technology/ai-problems-danger-chatgpt.html; accessed April 21, 2024.

26. Dorothy A. Greenfeld, "Same-sex reproduction: medical treatment options and psychosocial considerations," *NIH;* https://pubmed.ncbi.nlm.nih.gov/27077473/; accessed April 21, 2024.

27. "Gay Parenting Rights and Options Explained," *CoParents.co.uk,* April 6, 2023; https://www.coparents.co.uk/blog/same-sex-parenting/gay; accessed April 21, 2024.

28. Howard Fischer, "Gays can't have kids, shouldn't be allowed to marry, Arizona attorneys argue," *Arizona Capitol Times,* July 23, 2014; https://azcapitoltimes.com/news/2014/07/23/az-gay-marriage-no-kids-attorneys-argue/; accessed April 21, 2024.

29. Joe Carter, "Why Are Young Adults Increasingly Identifying as Bisexual?" *The Gospel Coalition,* February 27, 2021; https://www.thegospelcoalition.org/article/why-are-young-adults-increasingly-identifying-as-bisexual/; accessed April 21, 2024.

30. J. Peterson, "Gay comedian says straight people are 'boring' and reveals why being queer is superior to heterosexuality for one surprising reason," *Daily Mail,* September 26, 2023; https://www.dailymail.co.uk/tvshowbiz/article-12560283/Gay-comedian-says-straight-people-boring-reveals-queer-superior-heterosexuality-one-surprising-reason.html and Matt Walsh, "Super Straight: The New 'Transphobic' Sexuality, YouTube, March 9, 2021; https://www.youtube.com/watch?v=ENADjeOXYcA; accessed April 21, 2024.

31. Akos Balogh, "Why Christians Are Now The Bad Guys (And What To Do About It), *AkosBalogh.com,* 2021; https://www.akosbalogh.com/blog/why-christians-are-now-the-bad-guys-and-what-to-do-about-it; accessed April 21, 2024.

32. Brian Mann and Aneri Pattani "In 2023 fentanyl overdoses ravaged the U.S. and fueled a new culture war fight," December

28, 2023, *NPR;* https://www.npr.org/2023/12/28/1220881380/overdose-fentanyl-drugs-addiction; accessed April 21, 2024.

33. Ibid.
34. Michael Martina and Simon Lewis, "US wants coalition of nations to engage China in curbing synthetic drugs," Reuters, July 7, 2023, https://www.reuters.com/business/healthcare-pharmaceuticals/us-wants-coalition-nations-engage-china-curbing-synthetic-drugs-2023-07-06; accessed April 21, 2024.
35. Lori Robertson, "What We've Learned About So-Called 'Lockdowns' and the COVID-19 Pandemic," *FactCheck.org,* March 8, 2022; https://www.factcheck.org/2022/03/scicheck-what-weve-learned-about-so-called-lockdowns-and -the-covid-19-pandemic/; accessed April 21, 2024.
36. Nicole Sganga and Camilo Montoya-Galvez, "Fentanyl seizures rise at U.S. Mexico border—here's why," *CBS News;* February 3, 2023; https://www.cbsnews.com/news/fentanyl-seizures-rise-u-s-mexico-border-heres-why/; accessed April 21, 2024.
37. Matthew Green, "CHART: How Many Soldiers Died in Each U.S. War?" *KQED,* May 25, 2017; https://www.kqed.org/lowdown/22209/interactive-american-war-deaths-by-the-numbers; accessed April 21, 2024.
38. Hanna Rosin, "AI Won't Really Kill Us All, Will It?" *The Atlantic,* July 13, 2023; https://www.theatlantic.com/podcasts/archive/2023/07/ai-wont-really-kill-us-all-will-it/674648/; accessed April 21, 2024.
39. "V-safe Covid Vaccine Adverse Health Impacts," *V-Safe Data;* https://icandecide.org/v-safe-data/; accessed April 21, 2024.
40. Arya Devi, "McDonald's opens automated restaurant with no workers," *Edge,* April 28, 2023; https://www.edgemiddleeast

.com/business/mcdonalds-opens-automated-restaurant-with-no-workers; accessed April 21, 2024.

41. Eric Ryan, "No Human Employees at Fort Worth, Texas' Newest McDonald's," *1023TheBull,* December 4, 2023; https://1023thebullfm.com/no-human-employees-fort-worth-texas-mcdonalds/; accessed April 21, 2024.

42. "Amazon rolls out AI-powered image generation to help advertisers deliver a better ad experience for customers," *Amazon,* October 25, 2023; https://www.aboutamazon.com/news/innovation-at-amazon/amazon-ads-ai-powered-image-generator; accessed April 21, 2024.

43. "Self-driving trucks: We're in this for the long haul," *TORC Robotics,* https://torc.ai/trucking/; and "Self-Driving Trucks: Are Truck Drivers Out of a Job?" *ATBS,* October 10, 2023; https://www.atbs.com/post/self-driving-trucks-are-truck-drivers-out-of-a-jo; both accessed April 21, 2024.

44. Bernard Marr, "The 15 Biggest Risks of Artificial Intelligence," *Forbes,* June 2, 2023, https://www.forbes.com/sites/bernardmarr/2023/06/02/the-15-biggest-risks-of-artificial-intelligence/?sh=287c9f462706; accessed April 21, 2024.

45. Ibid.

46. "A Message from the Gay Community," SFGMC TV, *YouTube,* July 9, 2021; https://www.youtube.com/watch?v=ArOQF4kadHA; accessed April 29, 2024.

47. "Being Made In The Image Of God," *OpenBible.info;* https://www.openbible.info/topics/being_made_in_the_image_of_god; accessed April 21, 2024.

7

LET FREEDOM RING

We need to talk about freedom for a moment—pure, American, self-governing, democratic-republic freedom. Those words pretty much sum it up, but what do they really mean? Here's an insight.

When someone is in prison, they have a certain amount of freedom. They have freedom to pace around in their barred jail cell. They can do push-ups and sit-ups, write letters, even read books. If not in solitary confinement, they have freedom to walk in a line to the cafeteria for three meals a day while guards supervise. They have the freedom to go into the courtyard at certain times to get some sunshine and fresh air.

Prisoners go to work making license plates, growing crops, landscaping, and in the automotive shop. There are even libraries and classes for further education, gyms to lift weights, team sports like softball, basketball, and ping pong. There's a lot of ping pong. A prisoner can do a host of things while incarcerated. Yet all of it is just freedom within the cages. They are still in prison.

When a prisoner has served his or her time, however, and the guard turns the key unlocking that cell door and escorts them outside those penitentiary walls and fortified fences, we're talking a whole different level of freedom.

Unfettered from the walls and bars and fences and ordered routines, there is now freedom to make choices and create a life for themselves. Of course, we realize that there are enormous social and economic obstacles for ex-prisoners to overcome after their return to society. It's tough and part of the price to pay for criminal activity.

Still, though the new journey may be difficult, they are now free to embrace their inalienable rights that had ceased when in prison. What are those inalienable rights? As you read earlier and it bears repeating, according to the U.S. Constitution, "We hold these truths to be self-evident, that all men are created equal, that they are endowed by their Creator with certain inalienable rights, that among these are life, liberty, and the pursuit of happiness." When that prisoner walks out of prison, he has the right to life, liberty, and to pursue happiness.

Motivational speaker and entrepreneur Luis Centeno is founder of the highly successful Fit Results gym and fitness training company based in Chicago, Illinois. *Men's Journal* called it one of the "10 Best Gyms in Country."[1] Check them out online. What makes Luis's story so inspiring is that he started from scratch with virtually nothing except his skills after spending nearly a decade in prison.

Luis grew up in Chicago's drug-infested, crime-ridden inner city. "I started off on the wrong foot," he said, "and just continued with what was there," which was trouble. When Luis was 28, he was arrested and charged on three separate counts of drug possession, drug distribution, and possession of a firearm. He was sentenced to ten years behind bars. "I was like, 'Man, my life is done.'"[2] In prison, however, Luis had ample time to think about life, his mistakes, God, and real freedom. After finding the ultimate inner freedom, he pondered what he would do differently when back in society. He began to create a plan.

On August 11, 2011, after eight and a half years, Luis had served his sentence and was released to freedom. Life outside was brutal as Luis ran into one roadblock after another, one setback after another. "I got rejected in jobs, I couldn't even open up a bank account," Centeno recalled.[3] Yet he refused to quit. Being locked up had changed him, and he knew he didn't want to return to his old lifestyle or to prison.

One thing Luis knew well was fitness and how to turn your body into a lean, mean muscle machine. Working out in prison had been his outlet that helped keep him focused and sane. It was also part of his plan. This was America and he now had a dream. Some call it, "The American Dream."

Luis started hosting outdoor boot camps in 2012 with just a few clients willing to give him a chance. The results were so staggering that five people became 10 and 10 became 20. Word of mouth spread his success. "I was able to get me a very small apartment…in the downtown area of Chicago, where I was making enough money just to pay the rent," Luis says, "but that didn't matter, because I was free, and I had a plan."[4] Those 20 clients grew to hundreds. Soon Luis had a full-blown business, which he named Fit Results.

That is an amazing story of the power of freedom, but what does it have to do with killing America? Here's what. Living under the progressive,[5] socialist,[6] communist[7] ideals is the equivalent to living in a maximum security prison. In our opinion, you are allowed certain liberties and even provided certain necessities, but in eliminating risks and struggle, they eliminate drive, motivation, and a hard-work ethic. In essence, life loses passion.

Luis's story would have never happened under their system. He summed it up well: "[the struggling] didn't matter, because I was free, and I had a plan."[8] Read that again. There's something about the freedom to have a plan that makes the struggle worth it.

A caterpillar struggles to break out of its cocoon to become a beautiful butterfly. Without the struggle, its muscles are underdeveloped, and it can't fly and soon dies. Escaped slave turned abolitionist and great American leader Frederick Douglass maintained, "If there is no struggle, there is no progress."[9] Struggle and hard work are good and crucial elements in progress. It's part of the American Dream. In our opinion, those killing America hate the American Dream. They "Imagine," as John Lennon sang,[10] a utopian society[11] where everything is perfectly equal, God is out, no judgments or sin, no ownership, no corporations or competition, shared everything and everybody holding hands dancing with tambourines and flowers. The problem with that is it's not reality. Plus, it doesn't work. It doesn't take into account human nature, both good and evil. Thankfully, our founding fathers did.

Earlier in the book, I (Gene) shared with you that when I was in Russia that first time back in the early 1990s soon after the wall came down, I had encountered numerous people who were so oppressed and fearful that they couldn't even let their own spouses know they had become Christians because they might turn them in to the authorities. They had lived in the blanket of darkness and the prison-like iron rule of the government for so long that they had no conception of true freedom. It was like living in a penitentiary without windows because the government couldn't risk the possibility of some foreign voice of liberty standing outside waving.

Because of the open door due to the communist wall finally coming down, I was there with a team to launch some Christian television programing and teachings that would send a message of Gospel hope and freedom into that darkened land. The problem was because the people had lived within the bars and windowless walls of the government penitentiary for so long, not only did they have no real concept of freedom, but they also had no clue how to actually function in a free society. When the barred cell door of communism was at last opened, they just stood there, blank-faced, not knowing what to do.

For example, one of the things that stood out to me concerning our Christian programming was we couldn't talk about debt management, getting out of debt, or financial freedom because it didn't mean anything to the average Russian citizen. For 74 years they didn't have that. On the surface that sounds wonderful. I mean, who wants debt, right? But there was no free enterprise. Whatever they had in life came from what was allotted to them by the government, which removes all motivation for excellence and drive to excel.

The ingrained American, Western mindset is that you are given opportunities to develop your talents, work harder, build something for yourself and family, assume ownership. As you grow and refine your skills, you make more money and live a better life. Then, you give back.

The progressive left, socialism, disdains American capitalism. They like to preach that the free enterprise system is based on shameless self-interest and greed. But that's simply not true. Capitalists and entrepreneurs, those pursuing the American Dream, are no greedier than anyone else. In reality, the free market American economy rewards individual initiative, improves the lives of people, creates jobs, and promotes more giving.

Statistics clearly show that Americans, particularly entrepreneurs and churches, overwhelmingly give more and create more charitable causes than anyone else in the world. Significantly more than the government. Actually, government aid often obstructs charitable giving and makes it more difficult for Americans to give.[12] Still, the good people of America find a way to give more.

The socialist advocates want the government to provide, not the people. Freedom is about limiting government involvement. Another thing that founding father Thomas Paine wrote in his renowned treatise Common Sense is, "Society in every state is a blessing, but government even in its best state is but a necessary evil; in its worst state an intolerable one."[13] In its worst state, government shuts down initiative, vision, hope and true freedom.

Serving and giving back to the community has been part of the American mindset for generations. People had to pull together to survive so it became our mentality. Proverbs 18:24 (NKJV) tells us, "there is a friend who sticks closer than a brother." Remember in smaller communities in days gone by, family, friends and churches "raised barns" together? Americans came together for important life events such as the birth of children, illnesses, weddings, house moves, natural disasters, and homegoings. Nowadays, it seems like it's a big deal for someone to organize a "meal train" (signing up to bring a family in need a meal) or hospital visits during a major illness. We have forgotten how to care for others and, in a lot of cases, even our own.

So when family, friends, churches, and communities fail, big boy government swoops in to regulate what you need, from whom, how much, when you get it, how you get it, bureaucrats to patrol it, and charges everyone for what they decide is best for you, even though it's rarely in a personal, relatable, and timely fashion.

Take for instance the tragedy that happened in Lahaina, Hawaii.[14] A one-time allotment per family was provided by the government; after they lost everything, many of whom didn't have insurance.[15] And on a side note, our current government has sent billions in aide to Ukraine,[16] and the FEMA (Federal Emergency Management Agency) workers sent to help the locals are staying in five-star hotels at a cost of over $1,000 per room per night.[17] We don't know about you, but we don't think relying on and trusting our current administration to handle the care of our people is working like it should.

In early America, less government was better. People thought for themselves, worked for themselves, and raised and educated their own children. Homeschooling was big. You would be surprised how many famous and successful people were homeschooled. Benjamin Franklin, Thomas Jefferson, John Adams, George Washington, Thomas Edison, and Abraham Lincoln are just a few. Lincoln was almost completely self-taught, which most likely gave him critical and independent thinking, logic, and a desire to continue to learn as an adult.

One more note about Luis Centeno. His business Fit Results partners with the Angel Tree Program of Prison Fellowship, and he speaks in prisons encouraging inmates to stay out of trouble, and he hopes to start his own nonprofit organization.[18] He's giving back. This is what freedom is all about. Free enterprise with limited government involvement only works because it allows people to do what they do best and control their own destinies. Struggle is not eliminated, but it's the best system on the planet, and it is biblical.

In Matthew 25:14-30, Jesus told the parable of the talents. The word "talent" here is speaking of money, but in our case it can be used in our modern sense of "talent." This includes money as well other gifts and abilities God has given us. In the proverb, three servants were given talents by their employer, "to each according to his own ability." One was given five talents, one was given three talents, and another one talent. They were each expected to take what was given to them and multiply it.

The first two servants took evaluated risks, invested, and created profit. The third servant, however, was fearful of losing what he had and buried his talent rather than taking a risk and increasing what he had. In the end, the first two servants were rewarded with more, while what the third had was taken away. Bottom line, a major aspect of our inalienable rights given to us by God is the opportunity to take our talents and develop them or bury them. But it's our choice.

For many years, Russians didn't have that choice, so as we rolled out our programming we had to understand that freedom and self-worth was something they would have to struggle to learn and grow into. In the beginning, there was resistance to this new freedom, God, and the Christian message. All they knew is that once they could eat and they had food on their shelves in their houses, but now they didn't. And this quote was going around, "What was the name of the bomb that took food off our shelves?" Well, it wasn't a bomb. It was the fall of communism. They didn't understand that was a good thing because they had no understanding of free enterprise. They had no understanding of how credit works or creating a better life for themselves by working harder. All they knew was they had a job. And they did it and got paid sometimes regardless of their effort. They all got paid the same.

They had no motivation to dream and persist through the struggle to win. Like tee ball, there was no winning or losing and everybody got a tiny participation trophy. They suffered and lived that way for more than 70 years. But like Luis Centeno, who wants to go back to prison life when you are free and have a plan?

FREEDOM COMES FROM GOD

Our laws should protect our God-given inalienable freedoms, not control our ability to exercise them or pretend that government replaces what God has said. God is good. Because the

Russians' view of God had been distorted or completely eradicated by Lenin and Stalin, they had trouble accepting His love and grace and that He was actually for them. Part of keeping the communist ideology and rule alive was making sure the concept of God stayed buried.[19]

That's the direction we're heading in America, and the effects have been devastating.[20] This applies to all, but particularly to our younger generations. Wrote Pete Greig:

> If we're all just a bunch of highly evolved animals competing to top the genetic charts in a meaningless universe where our existence is of no consequence, what does it matter if some people get trampled along the way? We're merely cosmic beneficiaries of Tennyson's nature "red in tooth and claw": victors or victims in Darwin's survivalist lottery. It's Sartre's existentialism. It's Nietzsche's super-race emerging. It's tough luck on the losers, but so what?[21]

Yep. Take God out of the equation and America falls apart. With no God standard, what does it matter if a person identifies as a dog or a fairy or an alien? There is actually a term called "transspecies" for those who identify as non-human. What's even sadder is we are being forced to agree with them, and if we don't there will be serious consequences. A recent survey published by The Christian Post showed that "Nearly half of millennials think 'misgendering' should be a crime."[22]

With no God standard, what does it matter if drag queens and trans and pedophiles groom our children? What does it matter if fentanyl pours across the border potentially killing our children? With God out of our lives and out of America, there would be no lowest common denominator of freedom, and all people (particularly the up and coming generations) have is what they've been told for years and years by an atheistic,[23] America-hating educational system and culture.[24]

Pray for a revival of hearts! Only when hearts are changed does culture change. Sadly, even many of those who claim to embrace God deny Him with their ungodly policies and wicked agendas and with their votes. They have "a form of godliness" but deny its power (2 Timothy 3:5 NKJV). That simply means they have an outer form of moral superiority, but in their hearts and actions they demonstrate God's not really real or relevant.

Many of those trying to shut down the America we love are quite pious in their own minds and like to puff themselves up as moral, all the while celebrating evil as good, and condemning true good as evil. Once again, that's why our founding fathers did what they did in the establishment of our nation through the founding documents including The Bill of Rights, Declaration of Independence and U.S. Constitution. God knew the future of the world and was guiding them.

America was founded predominantly by Christians with Judeo-Christian values to be a "free" nation based on biblical principles. The mainstream media has created a term in their media language called "Christian Nationalism" to vilify that Judeo-Christian heritage and our patriotism. After witnessing the devastation of World War II and the horrors of evil governments, German Chancellor Konrad Adenauer told Reverend Billy Graham, "If Jesus Christ is alive, then there is hope for the world. If Jesus Christ is in the grave, then I don't see the slightest glimmer of hope on the horizon."[25] Adenauer committed the rest of his life to proving the resurrection.

In free America we have the right to try to influence you as an atheist to change your mind. And you have the right as an atheist to try to change our minds. We've seen friendly, spirited, and heated debates between Christian professors and atheist professors. Debate is not bad. Ultimately, truth prevails. Having healthy debate is part of freedom. Politically, we should be able to have the same type of debates. Unfortunately, what we see happening across the country, in almost every venue, is the shutting down of free speech and anybody who dares disagree. Some examples we have observed is in our media and social media. This is tyranny. In our opinion it seems as if culture on the whole despises God and His principles and Jesus Christ, who was God in the flesh.

Many American leaders do their very best to marginalize His name and remove the reverence, importance, and power in it.[26] Of course, pulling the strings behind the scenes are principalities and powers led by the enemy of our souls, satan himself (see Ephesians 6:12).

They realized that God was about freedom, that God created humans with free will and freedom of choice. That's why this beautiful nation was founded on God. Anytime God is taken out, freedom diminishes. It's just a fact. Look at the communist countries. Again, why do they hate God? Because the concept of God creates a realization of inalienable rights. The founders weren't trying to push a particular theology. But to those who cry "I'm offended," being offended is a right of freedom. Do you understand that? Being offended is not the same as murder.

Misgendering is not remotely a legal offense, let alone a felony. Mislabeling, or correctly labeling a person by the facts of science and creation, is not the same as physically assaulting them. Learning how to handle offense is part of maturity. If you don't like what's on TV, change the channel. If you don't like seeing somebody pray, go away. Don't pray. You have that right. This is America.

Take drag queens,[27] for example. There have been drag queens for years. If you're an adult and you want to be a drag queen, go for it. It's your right. But the moment you start taking that philosophy into the classrooms and start grooming and manipulating young kids, it becomes a problem. We have seen a drag queen on social media say that he couldn't understand why any parent would allow their child to go to a drag queen performance. Even he knew the difference between right and wrong for children.[28]

The moment you start pushing for laws that demand I embrace your twisted [perverted and non-biblical] ideas, we have a problem, and it is our right and duty and Americans to step up and stop it.[29] And when you as a drag queen try to legally silence my voice to speak against you, that it becomes tyranny. It's especially deviant when the government is using this as a weaponization to control.[30]

Those seeking to kill America want to keep us in their prison system. They want us to have freedom as long as it is within their domain and control. They don't even want to have windows that you can look out and dream. Because once you get used to their world, you lose the concept of what true freedom is.

The America flag stands for freedom. When we were growing up, we started our day at the flagpole reciting the Pledge of Allegiance. We honored the American flag and showed respect. As Paine said, "The cause of America is in a great measure the cause of all mankind."

Yet if you go to a main campus in America and wave an American flag and shout, "America is great! I love America!" watch what happens. A high school student who drove to school with his American flag flying proudly from the back of his pickup truck was asked to remove it by the vice principal of the school and the student's school counselor.[31] How messed up is that? Aren't counselors supposed to be helping support students? Are school systems more concerned about displaying trans and BLM flags?[32]

In addition, the current White House administration marked Easter 2024 as "Transgender Day of Visibility," and wanted to bestow them with civil rights.[33] We wonder why this nation founded on Judeo-Christian values has not had the Christian flag flown at the White House. There has not been a "Christian Day of Visibility."

It wasn't always this way, though. On April 25, 1976, the Chicago Cubs were playing the L.A. Dodgers and two guys ran onto the outfield and tried to burn an American flag. The announcer who was narrating the whole thing said, "Man, they are going to burn the flag. Can you imagine? Who would want to burn the American flag now?" But before they could get the flag lit, Cubs's centerfielder Rick Monday ran and swooped up the flag. The whole thing was being viewed on TV and on the stadium's jumbo screen. The spectators went wild with cheers and a standing ovation when

Monday made his move! It was one of the most patriotic displays in baseball history. It was shocking to most Americans that anyone would burn the American flag in America.

Fast-forward to today and look how different America is. Now they would say, "Well, don't interrupt the rioters they have a right to protest.[34] They have a right to riot, assault, and destroy." It's a different mindset that has taken over. And it's not just the flag. People have been arrested during pride events for reading the Bible on public property,[35] for praying on the sidewalk, for counseling someone on public property about keeping their baby,[36] for defending their property and lives from assaulting mobs.[37] Patriotism is seen as a threat.[38]

We agree with two of our former presidents of the United States of America that eloquently say that freedom always comes with a cost:

> "Freedom is never more than one generation away from extinction. We didn't pass it to our children in the bloodstream. It must be fought for, protected, and handed on for them to do the same," said President Ronald Reagan.
>
> "The cost of freedom is always high, but Americans have always paid it. And one path we shall never choose, and that is the path of surrender, or submission," said President John F. Kennedy.[39]

When the 56 men signed the Declaration of Independence, they knew full well that they were committing treason against England and they knew the penalty—death.

What kind of men were the signers? Twenty-five were lawyers or jurists. Eleven were merchants. Nine were farmers or large plantation owners. One was a teacher, one a musician and one a printer. They were men of means and education, yet they signed the Declaration of Independence, knowing full well that the penalty could be death if they were captured.

In fact, it was Benjamin Franklin who, after putting down his quill pen quipped, "We must indeed, all hang together, or most assuredly we shall hang separately."

Despite such dire consequences, the reality was that our founding fathers valued freedom and its promise for themselves and their posterity so much so that they would risk and pledge their "lives, fortunes and sacred honor."[40]

Signing the Declaration proved to be very costly. Five signers were captured by the British and brutally tortured as traitors. Nine fought in the Revolutionary War and died from wounds or hardships. Two lost their sons in the war, and two others had sons captured. At least a dozen of the 56 had their homes pillaged and burned.[41]

"Let freedom ring" should be our rally cry, and like President Ronald Reagan and President John F. Kennedy alluded, we must protect it at all costs, because many sacrificed it all so we could be free.

NOTES

1. Chris Malone Mendez, "These Are the 10 Best Commercial Gym Chains in the U.S., as Rated by Their Members," *Men's Journal,* June 16, 2023; https://www.mensjournal.com/news/10-best-commercial-gyms-us-according-members; accessed April 21, 2024.
2. Grayson Pope, "The Weight of Reentry," *Prison Fellowship,* https://www.prisonfellowship.org/story/the-weight-of-reentry; accessed April 22, 2024.
3. Blanca Rios, "Former prisoner, turned gym owner gives back to kids of incarcerated parents through Angel Tree program," *ABC,* November 26, 2019,https://abc7chicago.com/louis-centeno-fit-results-gym-angel-tree-prison-fellowship-christmas-program/5716256/; accessed April 22, 2024.
4. Pope, "The Weight of Reentry."
5. Progressivism; https://www.britannica.com/topic/progressivism.
6. Socialism; https://www.britannica.com/money/socialism.
7. Communism; https://www.britannica.com/topic/communism.
8. Pope, "The Weight of Reentry."
9. Frederick Douglass, *Selected Speeches and Writings*, "An address on West India Emancipation," August 3, 1857, vi.
10. John Lennon, "Imagine"; https://www.songfacts.com/lyrics/john-lennon/imagine; accessed April 22, 2024.
11. Utopia; https://www.britannica.com/topic/utopia.
12. Guinevere Nell and James Sherk, "Free-Market Philanthropy: The Social Aspect of Entrepreneurship," *Heritage.org,* September 16, 2008; https://www.heritage.org/markets-and-finance/report/

free-market-philanthropy-the-social-aspect-entrepreneurship; accessed April 22, 2024.

13. Thomas Paine, *Common Sense,* 1776.
14. "Lahaina blaze now the deadliest in modern U.S. history," *NBC News,* August 14, 2023; https://www.nbcnews.com/news/us-news/blog/maui-fires-live-updates-hawaii-lahaina-dead-worst-modern-us-history-rcna99635; accessed April 22, 2024.
15. Joan E. Greve and Dani Anguiano, "'I didn't get any help': Maui residents struggle despite Biden's vow of aid," *The Guardian,* September 2, 2023; https://www.theguardian.com/us-news/2023/sep/02/hawaii-fires-aid-fema-biden-maui-lahaina; accessed April 22, 2024.
16. Jonathan Masters and Will Merrow, "How Much Aid Has the U.S. Sent Ukraine? Here Are Six Charts," *Council on Foreign Relations,* February 23, 2024; https://www.cfr.org/article/how-much-aid-has-us-sent-ukraine-here-are-six-charts; accessed April 22, 2024.
17. Jolanie Martinez, "Images of FEMA works at luxury Maui hotels stir anger, but agency says it's there to do a job," *Hawaii News Now,* August 24, 2023; https://www.hawaiinewsnow.com/2023/08/24/anger-grows-fema-workers-stay-luxury-hotels-amid-maui-wildfires-disaster/; accessed April 22, 2024.
18. Rios, "Former prisoner, turned gym owner gives back."
19. "Why do Communist states (e.g. USSR, China) oppose religion so much?" *Politics;* https://politics.stackexchange.com/questions/8742/why-do-communist-states-e-g-ussr-china-oppose-religion-so-much; accessed April 22, 2024.
20. Robert Clifton Robinson, "When America Abandons God: The Signs And The Consequences," *robertcliftonrobinson.com,* June 30, 2015; https://robertcliftonrobinson.com/2015/06/30/

when-america-abandons-god-the-signs-and-the-consequences/; accessed April 22, 2024.

21. Pete Greig, *Dirty Glory: Go Where Your Best Prayers Take You* (Colorado Springs, CO: NavPress, 2016), 39.
22. Ryan Foley, "Nearly half of millennials think 'misgendering' should be a crime," *The Christian Post,* July 21, 2023; https://www.christianpost.com/news/nearly-half-of-millennials-think-misgendering-should-be-a-crime.html; accessed April 22, 2024.
23. Hannah K. Scheidt, "Practicing Atheism," *Oxford Academic,* June 17, 2021; https://academic.oup.com/book/39294?login=false; accessed April 22, 2024.
24. Amudalat Ajasa, et al., "They're teaching children to hate America: the culture war in US schools," *The Guardian,* February 16, 2022; https://www.theguardian.com/us-news/video/2022/feb/16/education-or-indoctrination-inside-the-bitter-fight-dividing-americas-schools-video; April 22, 2024.
25. Billy Graham, "What Is Most Important?" *Billy Graham Evangelistic Association,* April 10, https://www.billygraham.org/devotion/what-is-most-important; accessed April 22, 2024.
26. Charles Creitz, "Rev. Graham reacts to Biden leaving 'God' out of prayer proclamation: 'There is no one else to pray to'" *Fox News,* May 6, 2021; https://www.foxnews.com/media/rev-graham-reacts-to-biden-leaving-god-out-of-prayer-proclamation-there-is-no-one-else-to-pray-to; accessed April 22, 2024.
27. Drag queen, Merriam-Webster; https://www.merriam-webster.com/dictionary/drag%20queen.
28. Andrea Widburg, "Meet Kitty Demure, a drag queen who tells the truth about drag and children," *iOTWReport.com,* June 20, 2022; https://iotwreport.com/

meet-kitty-demure-a-drag-queen-who-tells-the-truth-about-drag-and-children/; accessed April 22, 2024.

29. Andrew Davis, "Drag queens take on Tennessee bill seeking to restrict their performances," *NBC News,* December 21, 2022; https://www.nbcnews.com/nbc-out/out-politics-and-policy/drag-queens-take-tennessee-bill-seeking-restrict-performances-rcna62125; accessed April 22, 2024.
30. Shannon Pettypiece, et al., "Biden announces sweeping vaccine mandates affecting millions of workers," *NBC News,* September 9, 2021; https://www.nbcnews.com/politics/white-house/biden-announce-additional-vaccine-mandates-he-unveils-new-covid-strategy-n1278735; accessed April 22, 2024.
31. Andrew Rowan, "Indiana school district goes viral for telling student to remove American flag on his truck, reverses decision," *WCPO.com,* March 10, 2024; https://www.wcpo.com/news/state/state-indiana/indiana-school-district-goes-viral-for-telling-student-to-remove-american-flag-on-his-truck-reverses-decision; accessed April 22, 2024.
32. Eesha Pendharkar, "Pride Flags and Black Lives Matter Signs in the Classroom: Supportive Symbols or Propaganda?" *Education Week,* January 25, 2022; https://www.edweek.org/leadership/pride-flags-and-black-live-matters-signs-in-the-classroom-supportive-symbols-or-propaganda/2022/01; accessed April 22, 2024.
33. Asheea Smith, "'Transgender Day Of Visibility' Per White House Announcement," *MSN.com,* April 2024; https://www.msn.com/en-us/news/politics/joe-biden-administration-marks-easter-transgender-day-of-visibility-per-white-house-announcement/ar-BB1kTIJ2; accessed April 22, 2024.

34. "The psychology of riots—and why it's never just mindless violence," *TheConversation.com,* November 15, 2019; https://theconversation.com/the-psychology-of-riots-and-why-its-never-just-mindless-violence-125676; accessed April 22, 2024.

35. Thomas Kika, "Man Yelling Bible Verses at Pride Event Arrested," *Newsweek,* June 6, 2023; https://www.newsweek.com/man-yelling-bible-verses-pride-event-arrested-1804888; accessed April 22, 2024.

36. Mary Margaret Olohan, "'Are You Praying?' Authorities Arrest Woman for Silently Praying Outside an Abortion Clinic," *The Daily Signal,* December 22, 2022; https://www.dailysignal.com/2022/12/22/are-you-praying-authorities-arrest-woman-silently-praying-outside-abortion-clinic/; accessed April 22, 2024.

37. Doha Madani, "Charges filed against St. Louis couple who brandished guns at protesters," *NBC News,* July 20, 2020; https://www.nbcnews.com/news/us-news/charges-filed-against-st-louis-couple-who-brandished-guns-protesters-n1234410; accessed April 22, 2024.

38. Christian nationalism; https://www.britannica.com/topic/Christian-nationalism.

39. Ronald Reagan and John F. Kennedy quotes: https://www.azquotes.com/quotes/topics/price-of-freedom.html; accessed April 22, 2024.

40. Scott D. Welch, "Our Lives, our Fortunes and our sacred Honor," *In Search of Liberty;* https://insearchofliberty.com/our-lives-our-fortunes-and-our-sacred-honor/; accessed April 22, 2024.

41. "56 and Treason: The Declaration of Independence," *Forest Lawn Memorial Park Association;* https://forestlawn.com/2018/07/02/56-and-treason-the-declaration-of-independence; accessed April 22, 2024.

8

STATE OF CONFUSION

Some consider Franklin D. Roosevelt (FDR) as one of the most liberal-leaning presidents in our history. Liberals liked him because of his creation of the administrative state. "The administrative state is a term used to describe the phenomenon of executive branch administrative agencies exercising the power to create, adjudicate, and enforce their own rules."[1] Conservatives disliked him because of his creation of the administrative state. The progressives of his time criticized him for his pragmatism.

Franklin D. Roosevelt was definitely a liberal democrat with views and policies many conservatives oppose. However, a true liberal, as much as we disagree with them, believes in America and in healthy debate. Many liberals embrace God at our foundation. On January 25, 1941, FDR commissioned the distribution of pocket Bibles to all the American troops. In the front of the Bible, he wrote the following letter:

> The White House:
> As Commander-in-Chief I take great pleasure in commending the reading of the Bible to all who

> serve in the armed forces of the United States. Throughout the centuries men of many faiths and diverse origins have found in the Sacred Book words of wisdom, counsel and inspiration. It is a foundation of strength and now, as always, an aid in attaining the highest aspirations of the human soul.
>
> Signed,
>
> Franklin D. Roosevelt[2]

We shared this letter and story to show you that what is going on today is much worse than mere liberalism. Today the Bible is banned in the military.[3] Chaplains have been reprimanded and dismissed for praying in Jesus' name.[4] Unless something changes, the Bible will never again be distributed among the troops. If a president attempted to distribute Bibles and wrote a letter like that these days, lawsuits galore would be brought up against him demanding an apology, like Americans United for Separation of Church and State demanded that Sarah Huckabee Sanders erase her children's chalk drawings of a cross on the governor's driveway in June of 2023.[5]

Actually, there has been an the effort to remove signs from military bases that say, "God Bless the Military."[6] The "cancel culture" philosophy has made an all-out attempt to erase any thought or mention of any conversation that is not in line with their absolute control and philosophies. We should not cancel anyone, neither liberal nor conservative. This is what free speech, which is guaranteed by our Constitution, is all about.

But as we have seen with Jason Aldean, a country singer CMT (Country Music Television) attempted to silence for his song,

"Try That in a Small Town," we the people have an increasingly low tolerance for this type of cancel culture attempts.[7] Instead of their desired result, it actually shot his song to the top of the charts.[8] Reverse psychology, so to speak.

These are things FDR would never have stood for. In our opinion, the progressive woke mob has hijacked the party on the left. This is why we have seen many leaders from the party on the left switching parties, such as Mesha Mainor,[9] because they know what is happening is beyond American and that their own party is facilitating those who want to kill America.

It also seems that many other groups of people (including Hispanic[10] and Black[11] voters) are leaving the Democrat Party for the very same reasons. Again, we are demonstrating that God and biblical principles have historically been at the root of the American way. When those principles are taken out, we open ourselves up to all sorts of confusion, and it seems to us that this is exactly what they want.

Face it. What's been happening these past few years is beyond the scope of our comprehension. I mean, who could have possibly imagined that those threatening to take over our country would be men identifying as women and women identifying as men, as they demand we address them by their pronouns of choice or be severely punished?

We could never have imagined an army of drag queens and gay activists invading our schools and culture, openly grooming[12] our children and proud to announce it while spitting in our faces. Who would have ever thought that men would want to breast-feed babies?[13] Never in our wildest. Who would have thought that the president of the greatest country in the world would appoint outspoken transgenders (identifying or pretending to be the opposite sex they were born) to highly visible and important positions, seemingly mocking us?[14]

It's like that high school charade beauty contest where the football team dressed up as girls in wigs, exaggerated lipstick and eye makeup, funny dresses, and high heels. The students and teachers in the gym got a roaring good laugh, but that was then—not anymore. Today they are dead serious. If it wasn't so tragic, it would be laughable.

In our opinion, it sure seems that a deadly virus and a vaccine have been weaponized. Didn't see that one coming. Nor could we have imagined how we have opened our borders, practically invited unvetted, unvaccinated criminal illegals to flood in, and then giving them voting rights and other goodies while taking away the rights of law-abiding, tax-paying American citizens.

It almost seems to us as if someone in our government is intentionally recruiting fighting-age males from other countries into ours. Ben Bergquam of AmericasVoice.news and FrontlineAmerica.com has personally told us that they are being assigned to certain cities throughout our country.

Though the government locked us down to stop the spread of Covid, it was never bad enough to shut down the border. We repeat, it was never bad enough to shut down the border. While it was demanded that American citizens have multiple Covid tests and vaccinations to move and work in our own country, these tests and vaccinations were not required for illegals coming into our country.[15] Let's talk about spreading possible multiple diseases within our borders,[16] to us, seemingly intentionally.

And who in their right minds would want to actually defund the police who protect us[17] as they simultaneously refuse to prosecute criminals and let them go free to commit more crimes? Such as the murder of police officer Jonathan Diller by Guy Rivera who has 21 prior arrests.[18] Well, it's people not in their right minds.[19] It's the antithesis of common sense. Worse, as we've pointed out consistently throughout this book, it's pure madness.

It's gone beyond just making us want to scratch our heads and say like the iconic Mazda commercial, "Sumthin's up." It seems to us that someone is pushing this anti-American agenda. That's why deep down you are more concerned about the state of our nation than ever before and ready to take action to overturn the tsunami of darkness and the plot to kill America.

In the previous chapter, we looked at the attempted flag burning during a baseball game back in 1976 and the difference in the response between then and today demonstrating how far we have digressed. Here's another example of our digression. We have a friend whose wife is a beautiful, well-adjusted professional woman. She was born a triplet—one of three—two boys and a girl. Because they did everything together, through preschool and kindergarten she wanted to be a boy. She wanted to cut her hair like her brothers and hated wearing dresses.

"I'm so thankful that my mom or a school counselor didn't sit me down and question me about my identity as a girl," she said. "My mom knew I was a girl, and I was going through a stage and didn't have gender confusion. When the appropriate time came, she taught me to be the girl I was and I outgrew wanting to be a boy. I'm so glad my mother embraced my femininity."

Let's face it, there are a lot of athletic girls and women out there who enjoy playing ball and lots of physical things who aren't exactly "delicate," but that doesn't make them boys!

Fast-forward to today, and a girl in that same situation could very likely be counseled by educators and her peers that she needs to seriously question her gender, confusing her. And, of course, all of it in secret from her parents while indoctrinating her against them, destroying the family authority structure set up by God. If the mother counseled her daughter that she was created by God as a girl and one day she would blossom into a woman, certain so-called "authorities" would threaten the mother. Again, you know this is no exaggeration.

Simple common sense tells us it's wise and right to protect ourselves, our families, and our nation against this tsunami of darkness. These attacks are generated toward our children and future generations. Attacks such as abortion, fentanyl crossing our borders killing children, dummying down the education system[20] and replacing it with perversion education,[21] addictions (alcohol, porn, drugs), sexually exploiting children (sex trafficking and pushes for "generational attraction" acceptability,[22] which is pedophilia), increasing deadly violence and crime, and unvetted, dangerous, life-threatening vaccinations.[23]

However, there is a factor they didn't count on that is turning the dark tide. Parents and grandparents are on fire and passionate about protecting their lineage! Yes, we are a free nation that respects everyone's individual rights, but we are not obligated to embrace ideologies and depravities that undermine the godly principles we were founded on: the Bill of Rights, the United States Constitution and the Declaration of Independence. Especially when it appears like an all-out plot, plan, and scheme to decrease population[24] and to eradicate future generations.[25] We are obligated to the next generation to turn this tsunami of darkness into the light of life. Herein lies the rub. They have abandoned common sense and want us to unquestionably fall in line with their wickedness, letting them determine what is best for us.

CONFUSED

It sure seems that everybody is confused these days. You ever wondered about that? Confused about gender, confused about how to address people, what's truth and what's a lie, should I get vaccinated or not, if skin color doesn't matter to me why am I being called a racist? They are attempting to rename pedophilia to generational attraction.

The Kroger grocery store chain employee guide instructs employees not to address customers as ma'am or sir. But it goes much further: The guide even suggests that employees refrain from referring to customers with language like "sir" or "ma'am." It also argued that gender and sex were distinct before going on to discuss those who identify as "non-binary." It defined the term as "a person who does not identify exclusively as a man or woman." "Non-binary people may identify as being both a man and a woman, somewhere in between, or as falling completely outside these categories," the guide read. It then listed some "gender expansive terms," such as "genderfluid," "genderqueer," and "enby."[26]

What is more confusing than that? Why is there so much confusion? Confusion is a symptom of a much bigger problem. Our identity is supposed to be in God by whom we were created. Throw God out and nothing is clear-cut; there are no absolutes. My truth is your truth. But that statement can't be true.

God is about order and freedom and truth and clarity. Satan is about confusion and bondage. This is one way you can tell whether any agenda is being promoted by the darkness. Gender-identity confusion is critical because it strikes at the core of God's truth. If you can stay confused, you can stay controlled. Do you think it's a coincidence that the LGBQT movement has attempted to steal the rainbow, God's sign of His promise?

Let's look at that. What is the one thing that God can't stand or tolerate? Pride. The Bible actually guarantees that if you want to go head to head with God, be in pride, He will oppose you! Remember though, this is not confined to homosexual sex. He hates pride and a proud, arrogant spirit. When you think about it, the way we all fall into error and sins of all proportions is when we think we know more than God (pride). When we think we can do whatever we want and there are no adverse consequences to our behaviors, we make ourselves our own gods. And that, my friend, is when you fall into all kinds of deception, error, confusion, and sin. As we would say in Texas, "A world of hurt."

God says that you're created a certain way, but if you say, "That's not true," you're in the community of LGBQT pride. If you're proud, God will resist you. The rainbow is God's sign of His promise, which they've attempted to hijack and pervert. The rainbow is about creation and the consequences of the severity of sin.

The LGBTQIA+ movement promises freedom and liberty,[27] but in the end it's bondage, confusion, and death.[28] Look at the statistics and look into the results. Confusion. But it's much deeper than gender. Facts are surfacing that Covid was a man-made and engineered bio-weapon created to drive their evil agenda.[29]

In the mid-1940s, at the end of World War II, Winston Churchill coined the saying, "Never let a good crisis go to waste."[30] He meant it to use the devastation of the war as a chance to create an alliance between Churchill, Stalin and Roosevelt for peace. The progressives have hijacked that phrase, like so many other legit things, and turned it into a tool to manipulate.

Rahm Emanuel, then chief of staff to President-elect Barack Obama, famously issued what has come to be known as Rahm's rule: "You never want a serious crisis to go to waste.[31] And what I mean by that it's an opportunity to do things once thought you could not do before."[32] Wow. Let that sink in. Every crisis, every disorder or tragedy, they use it to manipulate the public for their cause. Now evidence is coming out that many crisis situations have been created for just this purpose—manipulation and control of the populace (Covid, etc.).[33]

It seems to us like just about everything else, they've now weaponized confusion. The following piece went viral on social media. Although we couldn't pin down the author, or authors, it is thought-provokingly brilliant.

> So let me get this straight: we're a nation that accepts pornography but hates abuse. A nation that doesn't believe in gender but fights for woman rights. We're a nation that believes no child should be left behind, but we have aborted over 60 million. We're a nation where heroes have died so our flag could fly over a free nation, but then we give the title "heroes" to wealthy athletes who kneel in disrespect. We're a nation where political parties ignore the corruption of their own party while condemning the corruption of the other. We're a nation of laws yet we're a nation where that only applies if you're not politically powerful. We're a nation that has "In God We Trust" printed on our money but we're a nation where the ACLU sues people who make His name known in public. We're the "greatest" nation on the earth yet we consume more antidepressants than any other nation in the world. We're a nation that pledges we're "one" yet we're a nation of aggressive division. And we wonder why there's so much confusion?

The greatest nation on the planet supports open border policies that promote crime and give advantages to non-citizens—not their own veterans and citizens. This greatest nation is the largest consumer of sex trafficking according to the true-story, "Sound of Freedom" movie.[34] Citizens of America are nauseated by the two-tier justice system, and people are awakening to it and angry over the obvious gross injustice.[35]

Why is there so much confusion? Because that's what corrupt leadership wants—chaos and confusion. We believe there is a deliberate attempt to create chaos and confusion. But that's not what God does and that's not the freedom that this nation was founded on. We do not control others. America was founded on freedom and certain inalienable rights for individuals and minimal government.

Inalienable rights are individual rights that are not bestowed by laws, customs, or beliefs and cannot be taken or given away or transferred to another person. These basic rights are given to every human being by his or her creator, God. Often they are referred to as "natural rights."

Communist countries void of dedication to godly principles are manipulated, restricted, and controlled by government and not God, and the citizens have minimal freedom. That is what we believe those killing America want to do. It's what satan does.

But the word of God says, "Now the Lord is the Spirit; and where the Spirit of the Lord is, there is liberty" (2 Corinthians 3:17 NKJV). God is all about liberty and freedom to be who you were created to be. This is why the enemy wants God out of every aspect of our lives. Jesus instructed us to love God and love your neighbor as yourself, that these two commandments fulfill the whole law (see Mark 12:30-31).

In other words, when walking in love, laws are reduced because of love. We must have civil laws for maintaining order and driving safety, but those laws actually create freedom. Where there is an attempt to control, there is an increase in unnecessary laws. Even laws that promote evil at the expense of good. The weaponization of issues such as social media is all about political control and pushing agendas.

It's been investigated and found that those giving to Black Lives Matter (BLM) found out that their donations were used not to enrich everyday Black lives in need, but instead a mansion had been purchased.[36] People are not faceless objects to be moved around on a table like a pawn on a chess board. People are created in the image of God by God himself. When you treat people in a controlling, dominating, manipulating manner, you are going directly against the character and nature of God and against the person He created in His image. You are fighting against God when you seek to control others.

This actually describes the big picture of America today. There are two diametrically opposed forces going in hand-to-hand combat with each other. Good versus evil. If you are somewhat awake, the fog is lifting and you're beginning to see things as "clear as a bell." We believe the attempt is to overthrow the nation that was founded on a covenant with Jesus Christ and is dedicated to freedom and liberty. It appears every attempt is designed to pervert and bring this nation down to her knees, bowing to an unholy entity that has been trying to hit us with a tsunami of darkness.

We believe it is an all-out attempt to destroy anything made in the image of God. If you think about what's going on in the world today and all the mental health issues and problems, many are searching for their identity. Many have an identity crisis. Many do not know who they are or what they believe. Insanity and confusion go hand in hand. Get someone confused and they lose their sense of direction, their anchor point, their vision, their dreams, their hope, and ultimately their identity.

There is no true identity without a relationship and identity in Christ. Evil forces are pitting races against each other, promoting violence and hatred for those who have made a commitment to protect our lives (our police). Incentivizing killing[37] with Covid protocols by those who have taken oaths to keep us healthy and alive.[38] Injecting us with experimental drugs that are supposed to prevent a man-made bioweapon, but the drugs actually cause sudden death and do not prevent us from getting Covid, which was what they originally guaranteed.[39]

Our identity is supposed to be from God, right? And so, where there are no clear absolutes, then all this confusion comes in. We have a population that has been stripped of purpose and hope and identity—confused by a regime pushing an identity agenda, especially to our youth.[40] There is no true identity without a relationship with Jesus. That's why there is an attempt to remove God from the equation. The fear of the Lord is the beginning of wisdom and knowledge. If you're not in touch with the creator who made you and the instruction manual, then your basis for truth is eradicated.

Our friend Eric Metaxas said to us, "Freedom is unnatural. It is supernatural and most people in the world have not been free and if you don't keep God center, you're not free." We would say that the way America was founded was supernatural. God has been involved since the beginning. Take American freedom out of the world and the world would be a much darker place. When a tsunami hits, people just get swept away, sometimes hundreds of thousands. It's a horrendous reality of living in a fallen world. Yet it's a perfect illustration of what has been going on in our nation.

The first sign of a tsunami is what appears to be an unusually low tide. Although onlookers might be intrigued by this unusual sight, this major withdrawal of the sea should be taken as a warning that a tsunami wave will soon follow. In America, the tide of the influence of God has been unusually low for a long time. While the tide was slowly starting to rise, many of us saw warning signs. Some even shouted from the rooftops. But instead of preparing ourselves, America just couldn't believe it. Then, wham the monster tide hits, and it can be overpowering. That's what we see happening.

ARE YOU... (MOTIVATED, ACTIVATED AND DEPLOYED) YET?

Our values are truth (because it will set you free), honor (all people are made in the image of God), excellence (we serve the God of excellence and we work for God and not for people), integrity (God keeps His word and so should we), bravery (no greater love than to lay down our life for our friends), action (faith without works is dead), influence (make disciples of all people), leadership (the greatest among you is a servant to all), liberty and freedom (to set at liberty those who are oppressed), and unity (if two of you on earth agree about anything they ask for, it will be done).

God has impressed upon us to do everything we can to return our nation to its origins, one nation under God. We know the reason our country has always been exceptional is because we are in covenant with God since our founding. The first act by President George Washington was to strike a covenant between America and God.

Are you MAD yet? It's time for all of us to Mobilize, Activate, and Deploy: MAD.

- **Mobilize** – Assemble, prepare and be ready for service for God and for our nation.
- **Activate** – Organize and activate, or become more active, in what God is calling you to do at this time.
- **Deploy** – Position yourself and take action about what you know to do.

We all need to pray, speak up and do whatever God is telling you to do or that you know you should be doing. Some examples include running for an open school board position. We all have a big job to do—telling the truth, instilling hope, and providing steps to take America back for God.

NOTES

1. "Administrative state," *Ballotpedia,* https://ballotpedia.org/Administrative_state; accessed April 22, 2024.
2. "FDR inscribed Bibles for our troops in WWII," *Fosters Daily Democrat*, October 22, 2019; www.fosters.com/story/opinion/letters/2019/10/22/fdr-inscribed-bibles-for-our-troops-in-wwii/2470908007; accessed April 22, 2024.
3. Jim Daly with Paul Batura, "What Everybody Ought to Know About the Military Bible Ban," *Focus on the Family,* December 7, 2011; https://jimdaly.focusonthefamily.com/what-everybody-ought-to-know-about-the-military-bible-ban/; accessed April 22, 2024.
4. "Military chaplains told to shy from Jesus," *The Washington Times,* December 21, 2005; https://www.washingtontimes.com/news/2005/dec/21/20051221-121224-6972r/; accessed April 22, 2024.
5. Alex Nitzberg "Sarah Huckabee Sanders refuses to remove her kids' cross-themed chalk drawing at the governor's mansion, *Blazemedia,* June 30, 2023; https://www.theblaze.com/news/sarah-huckabee-sanders-chalk-cross; accessed April 22, 2024.
6. Chris D'Angelo, "Military Stands By 'God Bless The Military' Sign On Hawaii Base," *Huffpost.com,* October 14, 2015; https://www.huffpost.com/entry/military-wont-remove-god-bless-the-military-sign-from-hawaii-base_n_561d73fee4b028dd7ea595ad; accessed April 22, 2024.
7. Jamie Burton, "CMT Suffers Huge Blow After Boycott Calls Over Jason Aldean Music Video Ban," *Newsweek,* August 11, 2023; https://www.newsweek.com/

cmt-suffers-huge-blow-after-boycott-calls-over-jason-aldean-music-video-ban-1819181; accessed April 22, 2024.

8. Chris Molanphy, "How Jason Aldean Rode Liberal Outrage to the Top of the Hot 100," *Slate.com,* August 3, 2023; https://slate.com/culture/2023/08/jason-aldean-try-that-in-a-small-town-billboard-country.html; accessed April 22, 2024.

9. Jeff Amy, "Georgis Democrat Mesha Mainor, at odds with her party, switches to Republicans," *Associated Press,* July 11, 2023; https://apnews.com/article/mesha-mainor-georgia-republican-party-switch-democrat-a725f1c3d5e827a05a95eb178194f80e; accessed April 22, 2024.

10. "Why Hispanics are leaving the Democratic Party," *Washington Examiner,* September 15, 2022; https://www.washingtonexaminer.com/news/crime/2637264/why-hispanics-are-leaving-the-democratic-party/; accessed April 22, 2024.

11. Russell Contreras, "Democrats' big vulnerability: Why they're losing Black, Hispanic voters," *Axios,* March 13, 2024; https://www.axios.com/2024/03/13/why-democrats-black-hispanic-vote-republican; accessed April 22, 2024.

12. "Policy Brief: Yes, America's Institutions Are Grooming Your Children," *Center for Renewing America,* May 4, 2022; https://americarenewing.com/issues/policy-brief-yes-americas-institutions-are-grooming-your-children/; accessed April 22, 2024.

13. "Knowledge and practice of induction of lactation in trans women among professionals working in trans health," *NIH,* July 16, 2020; https://www.ncbi.nlm.nih.gov/pmc/articles/PMC7364529/; accessed April 22, 2024.

14. Will Weissert, "Biden picks 1st transgender person for Senate-confirmed post," *Associated Press,* January 19, 2021; https://

apnews.com/article/rachel-levine-health-secretary-4eee53439e9c2b4c27fcf4e7f572cb0e; accessed April 22, 2024.

15. "No, asylum seekers aren't required to receive routine vaccinations at the U.S. border," Erin Jones and Brandon Lewis, *Verifythis.com,* June 5, 2023; https://www.verifythis.com/article/news/verify/immigration/routine-vaccination-asylum-seekers-migrants-refugees-united-states-border-immigration/536-5a1ddfab-70f0-4af9-a676-987cd8627d00; accessed April 22, 2024.

16. Aria Bendix, "Chicago measles outbreak grows after more cases diagnosed in a migrant shelter," *NBC News,* March 11, 2024; https://www.nbcnews.com/health/health-news/chicago-measles-cases-migrant-shelter-rcna142801; accessed April 22, 2024.

17. Beth J. Sanborn and Darren K. Stocker, "Defunding the Police and the Unintended Consequences," *National Association of School Resource Officers,* November 9, 2021; https://www.nasro.org/news/2021/11/09/news-releases/defunding-the-police-and-the-unintended-consequences/; accessed April 22, 2024.

18. Joe Marino, et al., "NYPD cop, 31, fatally shot by career criminal during Queens traffic stop ID'd as husband, dad of young child," *NY Post,* March 26, 2024; https://nypost.com/2024/03/25/us-news/nypd-cop-shot-in-chest-in-queens-rushed-to-hospital-sources/; accessed April 22, 2024.

19. Zaid Jilani, "The Deadly Consequences of 'Defund the Police,'" *National Review,* February 1, 2021; https://www.nationalreview.com/2021/02/the-deadly-consequences-of-defund-the-police/; accessed April 22, 2024.

20. Keri D. Ingraham, "Dumbing Down K-12 Education," *American Thinker, Discovery.org,* September 10, 2021; https://www

.discovery.org/education/2021/09/10/dumbing-down-k-12-education/; accessed April 22, 2025.

21. Eesha Pendharkar, "Poll: Parents Don't Want Schools to Focus on Culture Wars," *Education Week,* January 31, 2023; https://www.edweek.org/leadership/poll-parents-dont-want-schools-to-focus-on-culture-wars/2023/01; accessed April 22, 2024.

22. Rita Kadora, "Ageless Desires: Unraveling the Mystique of Cross-Generational Attractions," *Medium.com,* December 4, 2023; https://medium.com/@RitaKadora/ageless-desires-unraveling-the-mystique-of-cross-generational-attractions-c598d1eb9590; accessed April 22, 2024.

23. Jordan Schachtel, "New lawsuit alleges Pfizer 'knowingly distributed' unsafe drugs to children," *The Dossier,* November 20, 2023; https://www.dossier.today/p/new-lawsuit-alleges-pfizer-knowingly; and Shaun Snapp, "How The Covid Vaccines Damage The Body," *Brightwork Research & Analysis,* January 25, 2022;

https://www.brightworkresearch.com/how-the-covid-vaccines-damage-the-body/; and Ian Lopez, "Covid Vaccine Injury Suit May Fuel Federal Overhaul, Litigation," *Bloomberglaw.com,* November 3, 2023;

https://news.bloomberglaw.com/health-law-and-business/covid-vaccine-injury-suit-may-fuel-federal-overhaul-litigation; and "Covered Vaccines," *Health Resources & Services Administration,* April 2024;

https://www.hrsa.gov/vaccine-compensation/covered-vaccines; and "We've Never Seen Vaccine Injuries on This Scale—Why Are Regulatory Agencies Hiding COVID Vaccine Safety Signals?" *Burningplatform.com,* August 13, 2021;

https://www.theburningplatform.com/2021/08/13/weve-never-seen-vaccine-injuries-on-this-scale-why-are-regulatory-agencies-hiding-covid-vaccine-safety-signals/; and "U.S. COVID-19 Vaccine Product Information, *Centers for Disease Control and Prevention,* November 6, 2023;

https://www.cdc.gov/vaccines/covid-19/info-by-product/index.html?CDC_AA_refVal=https%3A%2F%2Fwww.cdc.gov%2Fvaccines%2Fcovid-19%2Finfo-by-product%2Fmoderna%2Freactogenicity.html; and "Vaccinated People can still transmit disease, FDA and CDC officials admit,"

https://www.theepochtimes.com/health/vaccinated-people-can-still-transmit-disease-fda-and-cdc-officials-admit-5588370; all accessed April 22, 2024.

24. Isaac Maddow-Zimet and Candace Gibson, "Despite Bans, Number of Abortions in the United States Increased in 2023," *Guttmacher Institute,* March 19, 2024; https://www.guttmacher.org/2024/03/despite-bans-number-abortions-united-states-increased-2023; and Jody L. Herman, et al., "How Many Adults and Youth Identify as Transgender in the United States?" *UCLA School of Law Williams Institute,* June 2022;

    https://williamsinstitute.law.ucla.edu/publications/trans-adults-united-states/; both accessed April 22, 2024.

25. Nicoletta Lanese, "Fentanyl overdose death rates 'more than tripled' in recent years, CDC report show," *Live Science,* May 3, 2023; https://www.livescience.com/health/medicine-drugs/fentanyl-overdose-death-rates-more-than-tripled-in-recent-years-cdc-report-shows; accessed April 22, 2024.

26. Spencer Lindquist, "Kroger 'Allyship Guide' Tells Employees to Celebrate Trans Holidays, Support Bail Fund," *Breitbart,* August 31, 2022; https://www.breitbart.com/social-justice/2022/08/31/

kroger-allyship-guide-tells-employees-to-celebrate-trans-holidays-support-bail-fund/; accessed April 22, 2024.

27. Chai R. Feldblum, "Protecting LGBTQ Liberty and Religious Liberty," *American Bar Association,* July 5, 2022; https://www.americanbar.org/groups/crsj/publications/human_rights_magazine_home/intersection-of-lgbtq-rights-and-religious-freedom/protecting-lgbtq-liberty-and-religious-liberty/; accessed April 22, 2024.

28. Brian Mastroianni, "Why 36% of LGBTQ Youth Say They Don't Expect to Live to Age 35," *healthline.com,* January 23, 2024; https://www.healthline.com/health-news/why-34-of-lgbtq-youth-say-they-dont-expect-to-live-to-age-35; accessed April 22, 2024.

29. Shermaine Yee, et al., "SARS-COV-2 as an artificial creation: scientific arguments and counterarguments," *NIH, Journal of Medicine and Live,* Jan-Feb 14(1):118-120; https://www.ncbi.nlm.nih.gov/pmc/articles/PMC7982270/; accessed April 22, 2024.

30. Praseeda Nair, "As said by Winston Churchill, never waste a good crisis," *Real Business,* August 25, 2020; https://realbusiness.co.uk/as-said-by-winston-churchill-never-waste-a-good-crisis; accessed April 22, 2024.

31. Stewart D. Friedman, "Do Not Waste This Crisis," *Harvard Business Review,* November 25, 2008; https://hbr.org/2008/11/dont-waste-this-crisis; accessed April 22, 2024.

32. Matt Weidinger and Tim Sprunt, "The 'Never Let a Serious Crisis Go to Waste' Crowd Strikes Again," *AEI,* September 9, 2022; https://www.aei.org/op-eds/the-never-let-a-serious-crisis-go-to-waste-crowd-strikes-again; accessed April 29, 2024.

33. Joe Nocera and Bethany McLean, "COVID Lockdowns Were a Giant Experiment. It Was a Failure," *New York Magazine;* October 30, 2023; https://nymag.com/intelligencer/article/covid-lockdowns-big-fail-joe-nocera-bethany-mclean-book-excerpt.html; accessed April 22, 2024.

34. "Sound of Freedom" released July 4, 2023, by Angel Studios; https://www.angel.com/movies/sound-of-freedom; accessed April 22, 2024.

35. Richard A. Epstein, "Law For Thee, But Not For Me: Thoughts On A Two Tiered Justice System," *Hoover Institution,* June 22, 2023; https://www.hoover.org/research/law-thee-not-me-thoughts-two-tiered-justice-system; accessed April 22, 2024.

36. Gustaf Kilander and Andrew Buncombe, "Black Lives Matter apologizes after $6M California mansion purchase," *Independent,* April 12, 2022; https://www.independent.co.uk/news/world/americas/black-lives-matter-apologies-mansion-b2056313.html; accessed April 22, 2024.

37. Frank Ploegman, "Dr. Paul Marik on how government incentivizes hospitals to mistreat patients with toxic remdesivir," *Rumble,* 2022; https://rumble.com/vtfbcb-dr.-paul-marik-on-how-government-incentivizes-hospitals-to-mistreat-patient.html; accessed April 22, 2024.

38. J. Cama, et al., "To Push or To Pull? In a Post-COVID World, Supporting and Incentivizing Antimicrobial Drug Development Must Become a Governmental Priority," *NIH,* August 13, 2021; https://pubmed.ncbi.nlm.nih.gov/33606496/; accessed April 22, 2024.

39. Amy Sherman, "Biden says that vaccinated people can't spread COVID-19. That's not what CDC says," *Politifact, The Poynter Institute,* December 22, 2021; https://www.politifact.com/

factchecks/2021/dec/22/joe-biden/biden-says-vaccinated-people-cant-spread-covid-19-/; accessed April 22, 2024.

40. Nathanael Blake, "Why Some in the LGBT Movement Are Focusing on Kids," *Ethics & Public Policy Center,* March 28, 2022; https://eppc.org/publication/why-some-in-the-lgbt-movement-are-focusing-on-kids/; accessed April 22, 2024.

9

FORTIFYING THE WALLS

Walls can be a **good** thing. They protect and create security. They define boundaries and allow freedom within for people to safely live and move and develop. Walls have played a significant role throughout the history of mankind. In A.D. 122, in what is now northern England, occupying Roman forces constructed a stone wall, 12 feet high and 8 feet wide, stretching 73 miles from one coast of the island to the other. It's named Hadrian's Wall, and its primary purpose was to be a physical barrier slowing the invasion of raiders intent on plundering the country "for treasure, or slaves."[1] Hmm. Sounds familiar. We believe we have those set on plundering America, taking our treasures and making slaves of us.

Long before Hadrian's Wall, around 220 B.C., the Chinese had already built the mother of all walls the Great Wall of China, which stretched a whopping 13,171 miles. It too was for protecting against invaders. On a side note, we personally find it ludicrous that the country that built the most ominous and sophisticated wall for their country's protection is working with our government to destroy our borders, our walls, and our protection.

Erecting walls to protect from invaders seems to be a pretty common-sense concept. Why? Because they work!

Historically, a former president of the United States partially won his campaign due to his promise to build a wall on the Mexican border to protect America from invasion. Right now, from all of the people we talk to, overwhelmingly, the number-one concern and potentially a determining factor on how they vote is the issue of our current open borders.[2] Officials are deeply concerned that the open borders pose a national security threat.[3] The question we ask ourselves is why would anyone in authority intentionally risk national security?[4] Why does it appear that the gates have been opened to allow a tsunami of evil to flood in?

When the current administration came into power, they abruptly stopped construction of the wall and stacked hundreds of millions of dollars' worth of wall building supplies in huge piles simply to waste away.[5] But wait, a decision was made by the leader of the current administration to sell some of the supplies to avoid legislation that would require the materials to once again be used to continue construction of the wall.[6] What an utter slap in the face. Then they flung open the gates, allowing a tsunami of evil to flood in.

In October 2023, *The Washington Examiner* reported that "Enough fentanyl stopped at border in past year to kill every American 18 times."[7] Kill. Every. American. Not to mention letting in hundreds of thousands unvetted, potentially diseased, dangerous criminals and gang members.

We have to ask ourselves, "Why are potentially nefarious people being allowed to just walk in and potentially harm Americans when all that needs to be done is to secure the border wall?" It sure seems to us like there's a hidden agenda that is becoming more exposed each day. The American citizens who love their country are waking up. We need that wall along with strong gatekeepers to define and secure our borders and boundaries.

What's interesting about those who are killing America is they preach passionately, with great moral haughtiness, to tear down the walls protecting America and to defund the police while they surround their own homes with walls and fences and surround themselves with private security guards. The Pope, for example,[8] who condemned the border wall, resides behind the massive walls of the Vatican for his protection.[9] Practically all of those in Hollywood who are heading the charge against building a wall go home to houses in walled or gated communities with their own private security staff.[10] The general population cannot have walls while the rich and famous do.

It's like the climate control nuts condemning us for our much-needed vehicles while they fly around the world to their global warming conventions in private jets that burn considerably more fuel and emit way more emissions.[11] In China recently they have discovered abandoned electric vehicles, new, sitting in parking lots because some of them couldn't hold a charge more than six hours without recharging.[12] They just don't seem to be the solution for practical travel. But they are being touted by the elites as the way we must go.

The government wants to dictate where we go, how we get there, our own personal restrictions (masks,[13] distancing, vaccine status),[14] and how we cook our meals (gas versus electric).[15] They really would like to control all of our life decisions and whether we're allowed to have a life.

The hypocrisy is beyond belief. Don't get us started on the double justice system in our country—one for the elite progressives and one for conservatives.[16] You know it's true. You're watching it happen and are quietly thinking, "When will it be us?"

We are fed up.

Yes. Walls are good. God is all for building and maintaining strong walls. King Solomon, who built the temple wall and the wall of Jerusalem, wrote, "A person without self-control is like a city with broken-down walls" (Proverbs 25:28 NLT). He was talking about personal walls of self-control, but it was a metaphor based on a practical truth. When walls are broken down, bad stuff floods in. Why would anyone opt for no walls of protection?

God is a strong wall. "I will say of the Lord," wrote the psalmist, "He is my refuge and my fortress" (Psalm 91:2 NKJV). A fortress is known for having walls of fortification so those inside are safe.

God Himself instructed the wall to be built around the temple and the city of Jerusalem. Over the years, however, God's people let it fall into disrepair. Fractures, cracks, and holes were allowed to expand, and support structures were allowed to crumble. Israel's enemies were all too happy to contribute to the wall's downfall. After more than two centuries, the wall was virtually in ruins when Nehemiah stepped up to the plate. You know the story. We touched on it earlier. Let's briefly revisit it.

Nehemiah, though Jewish, had never personally been to Jerusalem. Born in Babylonian exile, he became a cupbearer to King Artaxerxes, which was an honorable position of trust. One day news reached him concerning the desperate condition of Jerusalem, particularly its broken-down walls. "The survivors who are left from the captivity in the province are there in great distress and reproach. The wall of Jerusalem is also broken down, and its gates are burned with fire" (Nehemiah 1:3 NKJV).

As Nehemiah heard about his people back home and their struggle to carry on the call of God as a nation, his heart broke. "When I heard these words," Nehemiah said, "I sat down and wept, and mourned for many days; I was fasting and praying before the God of heaven" (Nehemiah 1:4 NKJV). The desecrated walls around the city left the people wide open to Israel's enemies.

While in deep mourning, Nehemiah was moved to pray and fast on their behalf and then to take action, even though he lived more than 900 miles away. That's a long way on camelback, but it didn't stop him from obeying God's call.

Christian minister and theologian Frederick Buechner wrote, "Whenever you find tears in your eyes, especially unexpected tears, it is well to pay the closest attention. They are not only telling you something about the secret of who you are, but more often than not God is speaking to you through them of the mystery of where you have come from and is summoning you to where…you should go next."[17]

Nehemiah knew what he had to do and didn't waste time. He went straight to God and then to those with whom he had influence. God gave him favor, and with the financial support and military backing of King Artaxerxes, Nehemiah rallied the remnant in Jerusalem and began the task of repairing the wall.

The whole time they worked on the wall, however, the enemy ridiculed them and tried to stop them. "What does this bunch of poor, feeble Jews think they're doing?" the scoffers chided. "Do they actually think they can make something of stones from a rubbish heap—and charred ones at that?" (Nehemiah 4:2 NLT). Nehemiah's answer of faith was to encourage the people in the face of the opposition. "Do not be afraid of them. Remember the Lord, great and awesome, and fight for your brethren, your sons, your daughters, your wives, and your houses" (Nehemiah 4:14 NKJV).

It got to the point where Nehemiah instructed his people to work with a brick in one hand and a sword in the other (see Nehemiah 4:17). They were fighting by building the wall. The rest is history. God took those wounded, trampled-down people and rebuilt that devastated wall into an amazing display of protection and beauty. In a record 52 days, they pulled off something no one else could do in over 200 years!

Nehemiah's call to Israel is also a calling to us. Imagine what God could do through us if we came together to repair America? The enemy is scoffing the same sort of things to us. "We don't need your God or values. Shut up and keep to yourself!" "You're a racist hater if you love America!" "You're a domestic terrorist if you question the educational system!"[18] "You're unenlightened if you believe in traditional values!" Shall we go on?

THE HOLY SPIRIT

As Christ followers we have the Holy Spirit within us, and we can indeed be the walls of protection around our circles of influence and impact our nation. Of course, we need the physical brick-and-mortar walls with steel beams too. As we've mentioned, that's just common sense. And the tearing down of the southern border wall, along with other borders around our country, only further illuminates the insanity of those who want to kill America.

Taking a quick glance back at Ziklag and the tragedy that happened there, we plainly see that David and his men were the wall of protection. When they left to engage in the wrong activities, the city became wide open to the enemy that came in and pillaged their town, taking their loved ones as slaves.

Men and women today who are filled with the Holy Spirit's power and wisdom and love have to stand their ground. We can't leave our assigned territory. We must be the walls. And where walls are broken down, even in our personal relationship with God and other relationships, they need to be rebuilt and fortified. We take inventory through the Holy Spirit to reveal to us in our lives every wall in need of rebuilding and/or repair, whether that be in our finances, marriages, or the seduction of our children. Let us fortify every area that needs immediate attention right now through revelation knowledge received by Holy Spirit.

If we have weakened personal walls that allow ungodly influences in, we become ineffective in our assignments. "Above all else," Solomon declared, "guard your heart, for everything you do flows from it" (Proverbs 4:23 NIV). "Above all else." Nothing is more important than protecting your heart from the onslaughts and deceptions of this world.

One way we guard our hearts is by having spiritual walls fortified with the foundation of the truth of God's word. In addition, to protect your heart you must guard what you hear and what you see. As the adage goes, "Garbage in, garbage out." Your input determines your output and is the remote control of your thinking, your heart issues, and ultimately your behavior. From this moment forward, we need to rebuild the walls of divine protection, first around ourselves and our families, and then around our nation and constantly guard and maintain these walls forevermore!

Walls can be a **bad** thing. They imprison innocent people, like the infamous Wall of Berlin and the walls and fences around concentration camps during the Holocaust. Holocaust survivor Corrie Ten Boom wrote, "Love is larger than the walls which shut it in."[19] Bad walls attempt to shut in God's love and keep it from spreading. But God's love always breaks through—always.

The Berlin Wall blocked voices of freedom from having further influence on the East. The concrete barrier that coiled through the city halted the flight of those attempting to escape the brutal communist regime. Unfortunately, the wall worked in this case too. Chris Gueffroy, the last person who tried to escape East Berlin, was shot down in cold blood by a guard on February 6, 1989.[20] A year and a half earlier on June 12, 1987, Ronald Reagan had uttered those famous words directed to Mikhail Gorbachev, the General Secretary of the Communist Party of the Soviet Union: "Mr. Gorbachev, tear down this wall!"[21] Finally, Gorbachev got the message, and on November 9, 1989, the Berlin Wall came down.

Maybe, just maybe we should also be making a few declarations of what we want to happen. Maybe we need to speak to our walls, our giants, and command them to do what we need accomplished. The enemy loves to build physical walls that lock people up and turn into strongholds. The Berlin Wall was a stronghold of the enemy for 30 years. We can also be trapped inside emotional walls that become strongholds:

- **Wall of fear** (scared of reprisals)
- **Wall of inadequacy** (we're not good enough)
- **Wall of laziness** (somebody else will do it)
- **Wall of apathy** (what I do doesn't matter anyway)
- **Wall of identity** (we don't know who we are)
- **Wall of purpose** (we don't know what our part is in history)

Either way, God is also about tearing down walls. When Joshua and the children of Israel marched around Jericho and then blew their trumpets on the seventh day, God caused the walls around that city to supernaturally collapse so Israel could march in and claim their promise.

Yes, God is all about building strong walls, and He's also about tearing down walls. The key is having the wisdom to know the difference. There are times when walls must be torn down, especially if we are going to save our families and save America. The greatest walls we must tear down in order to obtain the freedom we seek in America are the walls in our own minds.

NOTES

1. Jarrett A. Lobell, "The Wall at the End of the Empire," *Archaeology,* May/June 2017; https://www.archaeology.org/issues/255-1705/features/5469-empire; accessed April 23, 2024.
2. Camilo Montoya-Galvez, "U.S. Border Patrol chief calls southern border a 'national security threat,' citing 140,000 migrants who evaded capture," *CBS News,* March 24, 2024; https://www.cbsnews.com/news/jason-owens-border-patrol-southern-border-national-security-threat/; accessed April 23, 2024.
3."FBI director wray confirms the border crisis poses major homeland security threat, DHS secretary Mayorkas stonewalls," *homeland.house.gov;* November 15, 2023; https://homeland.house.gov/2023/11/15/fbi-director-wray-confirms-the-border-crisis-poses-major-homeland-security-threat-dhs-secretary-mayorkas-stonewalls/

4. Nadia Schadlow, "The Erosion of Border Control and Its Threat to National Sovereignty," *Hoover Institution,* June 3, 2022; https://www.hoover.org/research/erosion-border-control-and-its-threat-national-sovereignty; April 23, 2024.
5. Mark Moore, "$100 million in border wall materials rusting away in Texas," *New York Post,* October 11, 2021; https://nypost.com/2021/10/11/100-million-in-border-wall-materials-wasted-in-texas-report/; accessed April 23, 2024.
6. Jenny Goldsberry, "White House auctioning off unfinished parts of border wall," *msm.com,* August 2023; https://www.msn.com/en-us/news/politics/white-house-auctioning-off-unfinished-parts-of-border-wall/ar-AA1fxkNP; accessed April 23, 2024.
7. Anna Giaritelli, "Enough fentanyl stopped at border in past year to kill every American 18 times," *Washington Examiner,* October 21, 2023; https://www.washingtonexaminer.com/news/2719723/enough-fentanyl-stopped-at-border-in-past-year-to-kill-every-american-18-times/; accessed April 29, 2024.
8. Kate Zusmann, "Vatican Military—Who Protects the Pope?" rome.us; https://rome.us/the-vatican-city/who-protects-the-pope.html; accessed April 23, 204.
9. "Papal security: New and old measures keep pope safe," *YouTube, CBS News,* 2013; https://www.youtube.com/watch?v=1ZOzgK0D4Cc; accessed April 23, 2024.
10. Tarpley Hitt, "Inside the 'Secret Service of Hollywood' That Guards Stars Like Post Malone and Jennifer Lopez," *The Daily Beast,* January 13, 2020; https://www.thedailybeast.com/inside-the-secret-service-of-hollywood-that-guards-stars-like-post-malone-and-jennifer-lopez; accessed April 23, 2024.
11. Ollie A. Williams, "118 Private Jets Take Leaders To COP26 Climate Summit Burning Over 1,000 Tons Of CO2,"

Forbes, November 5, 2021; https://www.forbes.com/sites/oliverwilliams1/2021/11/05/118-private-jets-take-leaders-to-cop26-climate-summit-burning-over-1000-tons-of-co2/?sh=49cab60b53d9; accessed April 23, 2024.

12. "China's Abandoned, Obsolete Electric Cars Are Piling Up in Cities," *Bloomberg,* August 17, 2023; https://www.bloomberg.com/features/2023-china-ev-graveyards/; accessed April 23, 2024.
13. "Executive Order on Protecting the Federal Workforce and Requiring Mask-Wearing," *The White House,* January 20, 2021; https://www.whitehouse.gov/briefing-room/presidential-actions/2021/01/20/executive-order-protecting-the-federal-workforce-and-requiring-mask-wearing/; accessed April 23, 2024.
14. Danielle Ivory, et al., "See Where 12 Million U.S. Employees Are Affected by Government Vaccine Mandates," *The New York Times,* December 18, 2021; https://www.nytimes.com/interactive/2021/12/18/us/vaccine-mandate-states.html; accessed April 23, 2024.
15. Samantha Maldonado, "The Future of Gas Stoves in New York: What to Know Ahead of a Ban," *The City,* January 13, 2023; https://www.thecity.nyc/2023/ 01/13/future-gas-stoves-ban-new-york-what-to-know/; accessed April 23, 2024.
16. Kash Patel, "Two Tiers of Justice," *RealClear Politics,* June 7, 2023; https://www.realclearpolitics.com/articles/2023/06/07/two_tiers_of_justice_149324.html; accessed April 23, 2024.
17. Frederick Buechner, *Whistling in the Dark* (San Francisco: Harper and Row, 1988), 105.
18. John Malcolm, "Are Parents Being Tagged as 'Domestic Terrorists' by the FBI?" *The Heritage Foundation,* November 18,

2021; https://www.heritage.org/crime-and-justice/commentary/are-parents-being-tagged-domestic-terrorists-the-fbi-justice; accessed April 23, 2024.

19. Corrie Ten Boom, *The Hiding Place* (New York: Random House, 1982).
20. Andy Eckardt, "Victims of the Berlin Wall never forgotten," *NBC News,* November 12, 2004; https://www.nbcnews.com/id/wbna6470285; accessed April 23, 2024.
21. John P. Rafferty, "Mr. Gorbachev, Tear Down This Wall!": Reagan's Berlin Speech; https://www.britannica.com/story/mr-gorbachev-tear-down-this-wall-reagans-berlin-speech; accessed April 23, 2024.

10

GATES AND GATEKEEPERS

Walls in houses and buildings have doors. Walls surrounding property, cities, and nations have gates.

These are places of entry or denial. Most gates have gatekeepers to monitor the gates. After Nehemiah completed the wall, look at what he did next:

> *After the wall had been rebuilt and I had set the doors in place, the gatekeepers, the musicians and the Levites were appointed. …I said to them, "The gates of Jerusalem are not to be opened until the sun is hot. While the gatekeepers are still on duty, have them shut the doors and bar them. Also appoint residents of Jerusalem as guards, some at their posts and some near their own houses"* (Nehemiah 7:1,3 NIV).

Wow. In other words, nobody was getting in at night, and during the day when the gates were accessible, anyone had to get past the gatekeepers to enter. Just as we are the walls and the watchmen on the walls, we are also the gatekeepers over God's covenant and purpose for this nation. The city gates were the center of the culture of the city. From the wall of the city gates, officials guarded culture. They gave the military final orders before battles and brought evil to judgment.

A lot of our social and cultural norms and natural boundaries, walls, and gates have been encroached upon, plowed over, and boundary markers moved. It is up to us to guard the social boundaries. The gates of influence only open one way.

The New Jerusalem has walls with twelve gates (see Revelation 21:12-21). You can't enter the heavenly city unless your name is written in the Book of Life. God is all about walls and gates. He's not just letting everybody in. Back in Genesis, God guarded the Garden of Eden and Tree of Life with a flaming sword and appointed an angel as the gatekeeper. There is a proper way and an improper way to enter.

In America, we welcome and celebrate all immigrants who come in legally, even while living here as they are going through the tedious citizenship process. Jesus acknowledged this principle:

> *Very truly I tell you Pharisees, anyone who does not enter the sheep pen by the gate, but climbs in by some other way, is a thief and a robber. The one who enters by the gate is the shepherd of the sheep. The gatekeeper opens*

> *the gate for him, and the sheep listen to his voice. He calls his own sheep by name and leads them out* (John 10:1-3 NIV).

Those coming across our borders illegally, no matter how nice and desperate they are, are thieves and robbers. Trying to sneak in and steal citizenship, they are illegal. It's just a fact.

NINE GATES OF AUTHORITY

We believe America has Nine Gates of Authority. What that means is there are nine primary areas of access over our nation. The reason we use the word "authority" is because gatekeepers have influence and power. They are the ones who control the flow of whatever is coming into our nation.

These Nine Gates of Authority are: 1) the home; 2) the church; 3) the educational system; 4) the government; 5) the media; 6) arts and entertainment, including sports; 7) commerce and business; 8) science and medical; and 9) technology. It's vital that the people of God realize the importance of their leadership outside of the church, particularly in these nine gates. If we had, we would not be in the dark tsunami we are now experiencing.

It has been all too obvious these past three years, beginning in 2021 that Christians have not been the leaders in these areas. In the medical field there has been a decline in saving and restoring life and more of a thrust to eradicate anything made in the image of God.[1] It has become evident also in technology that there is a continual attempt to get rid of people and replace humans—or anything made in the image of God—with machines.[2] Machines do not have free will and can be programmed and controlled. We see this in the implementation of self-service in just about everything, from checking out your own groceries to self-driving vehicles to deliveries by drones, etc.

There are many stories in mainstream media now about how if artificial intelligence grows unchecked, without proper precautions and regulations, there is a real threat of AI making humankind extinct.[3] Let that one sink in for a while.

Also, there are people now who are obsessed with technology, from monitoring systems at home so you can even talk to your pet from work, to Tesla cars that drive themselves, to the latest and greatest smartphones and smartwatches with all the upgrades. It seems as if some people are so wanting to be loved, accepted, and thought well of because they have the latest and greatest technological toys available. Unfortunately, these same people may be the ones who are wowed into accepting the microchip.

We were just watching a woman on social media who was ecstatic because she bought her groceries with the chip that was placed in her hand. It's so "easy"—all her banking, purchasing ability, medical records, all stored in the chip in her hand. Beware, people, that you too aren't sucked into thinking of only the pros of technology and not the cons as well. Just like the science fiction movies of old, they can and will be used for both good and evil.

And he causeth all, both small and great, rich and poor, free and bond, to receive a mark in their right hand, or in their foreheads: and that no man might buy or sell, save he that had the mark, or the name of the beast, or the number of his name (Revelation 13:16-17 KJV).

One more thing. The world thrust is for zero population growth—actually, "Let's decrease the population." But study after study shows the world is nowhere close to being overpopulated.[4] Overpopulation is a myth.[5]

When you think about trashing the nuclear family—the dad, the mom, the kids—who's the gatekeeper of the home? The parents. Who says what comes in and who's allowed in and what is allowed in and what's allowed out? The parents and the father are typically the protectors.

Marxists want the family authority structure destroyed. For decades we have been watching mindless movies and sitcoms that made Dad look like the bumbling fool—he should have been more sensitive, didn't know what he was doing, he was clueless. We've gone from Father Knows Best to The Simpsons. Homer Simpson, the dad, was an idiot. Add to that, the government rewards having kids out of wedlock and there is the recipe for destruction of the family.[6]

My mom used to say, "You know, you guys have it all wrong. Everybody's so busy trying to get the biggest house. Three cars, an exotic vacation every year, and you're turning your kids over to daycare from six weeks old on and you're shoving them in school and you're so busy saving the world, some of you volunteering for things or working on your career, staying late. You don't know who's teaching your kids." Mom was never more correct.

As gatekeepers, we no longer can make the assumption that individuals and institutions that have authority over our children are safe and trustworthy. It is increasingly evident that we must be more involved in every aspect of our children's lives to ensure their safety.

We're not trying to be harsh. This is reality. We're all about God's grace and we understand many mothers have to work; but if we are going to turn back the tsunami of darkness, we have to make hard choices. That will play out differently in each home, office, school, and church.

Let's look at the gate of education. We ought to be Christians with godly values who line up with the first covenant we had in 1607 when Robert Hunt's ship landed and declared that America would be dedicated to propagating the Gospel. Our values and education should line up with that. And we, the Christians, ought to be at the gate of influence for education and the ones saying what is allowed "in" and what is "out." "When the righteous are in authority, the people rejoice; but when the wicked rule, the people groan" (Proverbs 29:2 RSV).

The idea that Christians want to restrict freedom is a total myth too. Authentic Christianity is about free will for the individual, but it's also about stopping the advancement of evil agendas. There is a grave misunderstanding when people say, "I don't believe in God because why would He create evil?" God gave us free will. He gave us the choice to do what is right and just or do what is illegal and immoral. You wouldn't want a spouse who had to marry you.

God wants a people who choose to serve Him and follow His principles and precepts. He wants the best for us and has given us this great manual (commonly called the Bible) on how to live. He shares His heart and how He wants you to have a great life, but ultimately it is your choice. When people choose not to acknowledge Him and operate outside of His recommendations, they get the kind of consequences we are living in today. If you have an evil agenda, of course you will cry, "Hate!" That's what evil does.

Concerning the medical gate, the eyes of America have been opened wide. For example, everything that we've dealt with during Covid showed us that in the medical sector, much that is negative can happen in a nation with the wrong person in charge at the top of the gate.[7] Anthony Fauci shut down America.[8] The wrong kinds of people were locked up. Does it make sense to lock up healthy people?

Extensive restrictions on human activity, especially healthy individuals, is unconstitutional, let alone inhumane.[9] In Shanghai, people were screaming in their apartments, starving as they were locked in as part of a city-wide lockdown.[10] In other parts of the world businesses were shut down, depriving people their income and livelihoods.[11] People who weren't even sick committed suicide. Our kids became depressed. We've learned the power of organized medicine.[12]

If you are currently in the medical profession or you have been involved with people in the hospital, they would likely agree with our own personal experience of Teri being power of attorney (POA) for her sister who was in seven different hospitals in an eight-month period. It seems to us that our medical system is rapidly becoming like that of a third-world country and that is the progressives' goal.

On day one, the current administration closed down pipelines to make us energy dependent instead of energy independent. It's the same thing with the education system. Instead of pushing to excel in math and reading and real science, they push drag queens, critical race theory and perverted lifestyles.[13] They dumb down test scores in the school because only 37 percent of the seniors reached benchmarks for entry-level college courses.[14] Their solution? More aggressive teaching and tutoring? No. It is lowering the bar so that 87 percent passed.[15] We need to up the educational requirements. We ought to be the top-educated country in the world so we can lead the world like in the past.

Yet it seems as if decisions are being made to intentionally make this nation weaker and prevent it from becoming as independent and self-sufficient as we once were. There seems to be a direct correlation between a country's freedom and its citizen's ability to follow Jesus. Could it be that some of the countries with the least amount of freedom also are the countries where it's hardest to follow Jesus?[16] Could there be a push for government to replace God?

When I (Teri) was power of attorney for my sister who was battling a life-threatening illness, a nurse actually said to me, "You can refuse that drug. You can tell them no." On the other hand, we have been told that, "The doctor knows what's best for your child and you don't."[17]

Have Americans willingly given up our authority, often because we have not understood our rights as gatekeepers? We think we can't question. But in reality, we must think and question everything. Double-check your sources; get several opinions. We bought the lie that the medical "professionals" are infallible.

If you're like us, growing up we rarely went to the doctor. We had to have a broken arm or some serious bleeding before we went to the doctor. We hardly ever went to the pharmacy either. People just didn't do that unless very ill. And we drank out of the water hose too. Now, there's a pharmacy on every corner.[18]

We are a drugged nation, dependent on drugs,[19] funding the trillion-dollar pharmaceutical industry.[20] "The doctor knows best. Just do what the doctor says," we were told that growing up. We were told that the people in positions of leadership and authority were to be trusted and to submit to them.

I'm not trying to bash doctors or educators. I'm thankful for good doctors and teachers, but we must question them. A recent study revealed the "Majority of COVID Hospital Deaths Were Due to Untreated Bacterial Pneumonia."[21] So many people in the hospital who were dying, getting treatments, trusting doctors with their lives—and the doctors were using faulty and blatantly wrong data.[22]

One older man we know personally was literally dying from heart issues. He couldn't breathe and his pulse dropped to death levels. After being rushed to the ER it was discovered that he was overmedicated with prescriptions his "trusted" doctor had prescribed. When the medications were cut way back, he recovered fully and was like a new man. The medications were killing him! In so many ways, overmedicating is killing America.[23]

Gatekeepers are people who have risen to a place. Not only have they shown that they can be trusted in their own personal life and will take care and protect the culture and values that line up with the Lord, but they are going to be the very top echelon in their fields.

In Scripture, a gatekeeper was one who "guarded the entrance of the temple from defilements and impurities, faithfully administered the financial matters and maintained the temple property."[24] "This wasn't because God needed protection, but to prevent people from intentionally or unintentionally doing disrespectful or blasphemous things in God's house."[25]

> *The gatekeepers had been assigned to their positions of trust by David and Samuel the seer. They and their descendants were in charge of* ***guarding the gates*** *of the house of the Lord* (1 Chronicles 9:22-23 NIV).

You can take that same principle to America, where the church is the ultimate gatekeeper. The church's role should have been to keep the unclean out of education, to keep the forbidden out of the family, to keep all evil:

- Out of entertainment
- Out of the media

- Out of government
- Out of free speech

Instead, we abrogated our role to the government, the so-called medical experts, or the education system thinking that was the "higher good." It was really giving our authority away. When we give our authority away, we give control and access to someone else. We relinquish our protection and guardianship over who and what God wants us in charge of.

Here's another real-life positive example. In a community that we are aware of, they have a really good school system. It's a small community of about 25,000 people. The head of the school system is an authentic Christian and a godly man. He's also a top-notch professional. Filtered underneath him is an umbrella of other Christian leaders he put into place. We say, "He put in," but it was the community under his influence who put them in. We're talking godly, powerful Christians who are in key places in that school system. They are gatekeepers.

This leader of the school system, as well as the others, rose to the top because of his excellence. He didn't start off one day at 20 years old as the head of the school system. He inhabited where he was to the full extent he was given.

And that's really just like re-digging the wells. The first shovel doesn't mean you're at the water. You have to keep going and going. If we all do our part, some will get to the top of the gate before the others. But the reality is, if we're not even digging, we're sitting waiting for somebody else to do the digging.

THE CREAM STILL RISES TO THE TOP

Despite everything we see going on, the cream rises to the top. If you are excellent, more will be expected of you, and if you are faithful with what has been given to you, you will have more opportunity than ever before. "For whoever has will be given more, and they will have an abundance. Whoever does not have, even what they have will be taken from them" (Matthew 25:29 NIV). That sounds harsh, but in today's language it's saying, "If you are industrious with what you've been entrusted, you'll be given more; but if you are not, what you have will be taken away."

Excellence in all of those Nine Gates of Authority is still going to be rewarded. There is certainly a cancel culture out there, but ultimately excellence rises to the top. This is why they are trying to get rid of excellence.[26] So your job as a gatekeeper is not just your own personal thing, but to excel in whatever gifts and talents that God has given you. You keep taking on more responsibility as you rise to the top, and you do your best to bring others up to your level for the glory of the Lord.

A gatekeeper is to set society's cultural norms. We're to set what's right and what's wrong because we're doing it according to God's word. We have had culture dictate and shove things down our throat. If we don't stand up, we are just as guilty of killing America because we're not doing anything.

Kenneth Copeland said this a long time ago and it was something that really stuck. He was talking about voting. "When you vote, your vote is your seed, and God doesn't do anything without a seed. When you don't sow it, you have sown to your enemy."[27] If you decide to not vote, you voted. You have a part in every evil thing the person does who is elected. We must understand the power of our vote as Americans and as believers. It's our responsibility to vote.

YOUR CIRCLE OF INFLUENCE

Every person has a circle of influence. If you notice in the Nehemiah passage at the beginning of this chapter, there were gatekeepers, but there were also guards close to the homes and families. This is where most people live. Everybody has a circle of influence that God has given them. History is full of the ones who stood up.

Rosa Parks helped initiate the civil rights movement in the United States in 1955 when she refused to give up her seat to a white man on a Montgomery, Alabama, bus. Rosa's actions inspired the leaders of the local Black community to organize the Montgomery Bus Boycott, which was led by Reverend Martin Luther King Jr. The boycott lasted more than a year. It ended when the U.S. Supreme Court ruled that bus segregation was unconstitutional.[28] Look what the result was. That's the power of the one.

Your circle of influence begins with where you are right now—on a bus, in a classroom, in a hospital room, at a ballgame, the grocery store, in your living room. We all have an opportunity to stand up, and we have been fed a lie that we don't matter.[29] If we don't speak out, the balance of someone's life is literally on the line.

Mom and dad feel like they're out of touch because of the cultural differences. The truth is, we do matter. Grandmothers and grandpas matter too. In our own family, we have said that if their grandparents weren't in heaven, some of the stupid things our children are doing, they wouldn't have even considered. Mind you, not out of fear, but out of love for not disappointing them and letting them down. Why would it be so important in Scripture to leave an inheritance for your children's children?[30] Because we're supposed to do that for our families.

Most revivals started with one person who said, "I'll stand up. I just want to seek God more than anybody else. I want to be an example of His love for me." We can say that in the secular world too. One person decided to stand up or stay seated, and she changed a nation.

We've been fed a lie that somehow we as individuals don't matter and we should conform to group thinking.[31] And the truth is we do matter as individuals. The wonderful thing about this country is our founding fathers took great pains to make sure we weren't a democracy, which is basically mob rule.

The United States is not a mob-rule democracy. We're a democratic republic. And most people don't understand the difference. This nation is built on the importance of the individual, not the masses. Communism is based on the "greater good"; the individual gives up rights for the masses. This is not biblical, and it never works.

The belief that "I don't really matter" is one of the biggest lies that we've bought in the Christian world. "Well, who am I? What does my $20 a month do? Who am I? I mean, my neighbor has a bigger car than mine, and their house looks better, and their kids look perfect. Why should I meet them? Who am I? What am I? I'm really not that important." And the more the enemy of our souls beats us down with that false belief, the more we don't do anything.

A lot of this thinking is because we get so caught up looking at ourselves and we believe that we don't have anything to offer. And the truth is, we all absolutely do have something to offer, and everybody else will see that we do when we get up and do it. Go do it!

In the kid's movie "Finding Nemo,"[32] Nemo was caught in a net with a large school of fish. They were being brought up in a huge net for the kill. Then one of the fish got a brave idea, they all started swimming together toward the bottom of the net. The force of the "team" broke the net, almost took out the boat, and produced freedom for them all. Because they all worked together, they created a tsunami of light and goodness to produce their freedom.

Many of us don't understand who we are and what we carry; we are supposed to be influencing people all the time for Christ. Let's say you are a plumber and you're at somebody's house fixing a pipe. While there, you're on your phone, you don't greet the people other than an initial hello, you don't talk to them, you don't have eye contact, you're not friendly. You just get in and get out. You just lost your opportunity to affect somebody for God.

How do you climb a mountain? You start. You take one step at a time. We can be gatekeepers by taking one step and thinking continuously. You are a watchman like on Nehemiah's wall. You protect, you know your purpose, your identity, and your authority. You are courageous, knowing you have generations to protect. You don't give up your post or authority.

Take possession and control of your gate of authority. Together, we will turn back the tsunami of darkness and stop the killing of America.

NOTES

1. L. Sue Baugh, "assisted suicide," March 26, 2024; https://www.britannica.com/topic/assisted-suicide; accessed April 23, 2024.
2. Matt O'Brien, "Beyond Elon Musk's Optimus, robot startups see huge market," *Fortune,* November 5, 2023; https://fortune.com/2023/11/05/when-will-robots-replace-humans-startups-elon-musk-humanoids-optimus/; accessed April 23, 2024.
3. Matt Egan, "AI could pose 'extinction-level' threat to humans and the US must intervene, State Dept.-commissioned report warns; *CNN.com,* March 12, 2024; https://www.cnn.com/2024/03/12/business/artificial-intelligence-ai-report-extinction/index.html; accessed April 23, 2024.
4. Anthony Cilluffo and Neil G. Ruiz, "World's population is projected to nearly stop growing by the end of the century," *Pew Research Center,* June 17, 2019; https://www.pewresearch.org/ short-reads/2019/06/17/

worlds-population-is-projected-to-nearly-stop-growing-by-the-end-of-the-century; accessed April 23, 2024.

5. Jared Wolf, "3 clear reasons why overpopulation is a myth," *Sustainable Review,* January 29, 2024, https://sustainablereview.com/overpopulation-is-a-myth; accessed April 23, 2024.

6. Emma Johnson, "Government help for single mothers with low or no income: 18 assistance programs," *wealthysinglemommy.com,* March 26, 2024; https://www.wealthysinglemommy.com/government-assistance/; accessed April 23, 2024.

7. "FACT CHECK: Anthony Fauci Falsely Claims He Never Recommended Shutdowns to Fight Coronavirus," *AllSides,* July 27, 2022; https://www.allsides.com/news/2022-07-27-2106/fact-check-anthony-fauci-falsely-claims-he-never-recommended-shutdowns-fight; accessed April 23, 2024.

8. David Wallace-Wells, "Dr. Fauci Looks Back: Something Clearly Went Wrong," *The New York Times,* April 24, 2023; https://www.nytimes.com/interactive/2023/04/24/magazine/dr-fauci-pandemic.html; accessed April 23, 2024.

9. Steve Dewey, "Covid-19 Lockdowns Violate the US Constitution," *American Institute for Economic Research,* March 9, 2021; https://www.aier.org/article/covid-19-lockdowns-violate-the-us-constitution/; accessed April 23, 2024.

10. Steven Jiang, "Hunger and anger in Shanghai's unending lockdown nightmare," *CNN.com,* April 19, 2022; https://www.cnn.com/2022/04/19/china/shanghai-covid-lockdown-nightmare-intl-dst-hnk/index.html; accessed April 23, 2024.

11. Hanna Dingel, et al., "The state of the U.S. health system in 2022 and the outlook for 2023," *Health System Tracker,* December 22, 2022; https://www.healthsystemtracker.org/brief/

the-state-of-the-u-s-health-system-in-2022-and-the-outlook-for-2023/; accessed April 23, 2024.

12. Iman Ghosh, "Mapped: The State of Small Business Recovery in America," *Visual Capitalist,* April 28, 2021; https://www.visualcapitalist.com/mapped-the-state-of-small-business-recovery-in-america/; accessed April 23, 2024.
13. Laura Meckler, "Public education is facing a crisis of epic proportions," *The Washington Post,* January 30, 2022; https://www.washingtonpost.com/education/2022/01/30/public-education-crisis-enrollment-violence/; accessed April 23, 2024.
14. Louis Jacobson, "Tommy Tuberville, 'Half the kids in this country, when they graduate, can't read their diploma,'" *Politifact The Poynter Institute,* March 20, 2023; https://www.politifact.com/factchecks/2023/mar/20/tommy-tuberville/can-half-us-high-school-graduates-not-read-their-d/; accessed April 23, 2024.
15. "Public High School Graduation Rates," *National Center for Education Statistics,* May 2023; https://nces.ed.gov/programs/coe/indicator/coi/high-school-graduation-rates; accessed April 23, 2024.
16. "The 50 Countries Where It's Most Dangerous to Follow Jesus in 2021," *Christianity Today,* January 13, 2021; https://www.christianitytoday.com/news/2021/january/christian-persecution-2021-countries-open-doors-watch-list.html; accessed April 23, 2024.
17. "Pediatric Decision Making Recommendations Empower Parents, Emphasize Many Interests Impacting Kids," *University of Rochester Medical Center,* August 21, 2023; https://www.urmc.rochester.edu/news/story/pediatric-decision-making

-recommendations-empower-parents-emphasize-many-interests-impacting-kids; accessed April 23, 2024.

18. "A drugstore on every corner: Turning points in community pharmacy," *Drug Topics,* March 10, 2016; https://www.drugtopics.com/view/drugstore-every-corner-turning-points-community-pharmacy; accessed April 23, 2024.

19. Damon Linker, "Why are Americans drugging themselves to death?" *The Week,* November 19, 2021; https://theweek.com/drugs/1007279/why-are-americans-drugging-themselves-to-death; accessed April 23, 2024.

20. Matej Mikulic, "Global Pharmaceutical Industry Statistics and Facts," *Statista.com;* January 10, 2024; https://www.statista.com/topics/1764/global-pharmaceutical-industry/#topicOverview and Terry Gross, "How U.S. Health Care Became Big Business," *NPR,* April 10, 2017;

    https://www.npr.org/sections/health-shots/2017/04/10/523005353/how-u-s-health-care-became-big-business and Dr. Thomas Pollak, "Time to move on from 'doctor knows best', say experts, as study finds clinicians rank patient views as least important in diagnosis," King's College London, December 18, 2023;

    https://www.kcl.ac.uk/news/time-to-move-on-from-doctor-knows-best-say-experts-as-study-finds-clinicians-rank-patient-views-as-least-important-in-diagnosis; all accessed April 23, 2024.

21. James Lyons-Weiler, "Majority of COVID Hospital Deaths Were Due to Untreated Bacterial Pneumonia," *The Epoch Times,* May 28, 2023; https://www.theepochtimes.com/mkt_app/health/majority-of-covid-hospital-deaths-were-due-to

-untreated-bacterial-pneumonia-5294482; accessed April 23, 2024.

22. James Lyons-Weiler, "Majority of COVID Hospital Deaths Were Due to Untreated Bacterial Pneumonia," *TheDefender,* May 17, 2023; https://childrenshealthdefense.org/defender/covid-hospital-deaths-bacterial-pneumonia/; accessed April 23, 2024.
23. Shannon Brownlee and Judith Garber, "Overprescribed: High cost isn't America's only drug problem," *STAT,* April 2, 2019; https://www.statnews.com/2019/04/02/overprescribed-americas-other-drug-problem/; accessed April 23, 2024.
24. F. Wayne Mac Leod, *Gatekeepers of the Temple: An Examination of the Role of Gatekeeper in the Old Testament and Its Lessons for the Christian Life Today* (July 2019).
25. Bradley Baurain, "Daily Devotional: Gatekeepers Of The Temple," *Today in the Word,* March 8, 2020, https://www.todayintheword.org/daily-devotional/gatekeepers-of-the-temple; accessed April 23, 2024.
26. Peter Turchin, "America Is Headed Toward Collapse," *The Atlantic,* June 2, 2023; https://www.theatlantic.com/ideas/archive/2023/06/us-societal-trends-institutional-trust-economy/674260/; accessed April 23, 2024.
27. Kenneth Copeland, "Your Ballot Is Your Seed," *Kenneth Copeland Ministries,* September 27, 2022; https://blog.kcm.org/your-ballot-is-your-seed/; accessed April 23, 2024.
28. "Rosa Parks," *History.com,* February 20, 2024; https://www.history.com/topics/black-history/rosa-parks; accessed April 23, 2024.
29. Colonel Mickey Addison, "Ronald Reagan and Character and Leadership, *mickeyaddison.com,* February 2013; https://www

.mickeyaddison.com/2013/02/19/ronald-reagan-on-character-leadership/; accessed April 23, 2024.

30. See Romans 8:17; Proverbs 13:22; Exodus 32:13; Leviticus 20:24; Ephesians 1:18; Hebrews 9:15; 1 Peter 1:3-4.
31. Leo, "What Is Conformity? Understanding the Psychology Behind Our Need to Fit In," *Psychologily,* October 26, 2023; https://psychologily.com/what-is-conformity/; accessed April 23, 2024.
32. "Finding Nemo," released May 30, 2003, *Disney;* https://movies.disney.com/finding-nemo; accessed April 23, 2024.

11

CALLED TO OCCUPY

We previously read that Frederick Douglass said, "If there is no struggle, there is no progress."[1] That's true. However, he also said, "I prayed for freedom for twenty years, but received no answer until I prayed with my legs."[2] Frederick Douglass prayed and stood against slavery for years. He did everything he could do spiritually and verbally to end slavery and be free, but there came a point when his struggle for progress meant taking a calculated risk of action. By faith, he had to step outside of his comfort zone and make a run for it, trusting God as he went.

There are two ways the Lord moves the seemingly insurmountable mountains in our lives. He may supernaturally remove the mountain. We've seen that happen. We know that our God is the God of miracles. More often than not, though, God hands us a shovel and says, "Trust me with each shovelful for empowerment as you dig through to the other side." Or he drops us a rope and says, "Hold on and start climbing. I'll strengthen you and protect you from the arrows flying toward you as you're advancing to the peak."

Being empowered to tunnel through or to scale the rocky cliff is just as supernatural as God removing the mountain. Jesse Duplantis said to us, "All that you cannot do, God will do. All that you can do, God will never do." Faith can be standing firm and not moving. Faith can also be securing our laces and running with all our might. Just like it is wise to understand when walls need to be built and when walls need to be torn down, it takes wisdom to know when God wants us to stand firm and when God wants us to get moving.

Drawing that line in the sand, standing your ground, and refusing to move is a form of action. Other times, we are called to cross over the enemy's lines and sprint forward in faith, trusting God to direct our steps.

When we run, however, we can't run timidly. It's either "Move fast with power, strength, and stamina!" or "Get killed!" A motivational quote that has circulated for several years with no known original author says, "Every day in Africa a gazelle wakes up. It knows it must run faster than the fastest lion or it will be killed. Every morning a lion wakes up. It knows that it must outrun the slowest gazelle, or it will starve to death. It doesn't matter whether you are a lion or a gazelle. When the sun comes up, you better be running."

I'm quite sure when Frederick Douglass was escaping slavery, trudging through woods and farmland and crossing rivers, he may have glanced back over his shoulder occasionally, but he was running fast and focused, using all his God-given faculties and discernment to keep from being captured. With an undivided heart, he was running sold out. Slavery was wrong and he was never turning back, never. He would die first.

After David delivered lunch that day and then killed Goliath, the pursuit really began. As he was running from Saul for years, hiding in caves, and pursuing his divine calling to one day be king, he cried out to God, "give me an undivided heart" (Psalm 86:11 NIV). This should be our cry too. David prayed those specific words because he understood that it is impossible to walk in God's favor and do what he was meant to do with a divided heart.

Is your heart divided? Saving America is a divine calling, but we can't if our hearts are divided—divided in our own personal walk with God and divided as fellow soldiers in this battle. In his last public speech in 1799, Patrick Henry declared with great passion, "Let us trust God and our better judgment to set us right hereafter. United we stand, divided we fall."[3] This is yet another reminder that our founding fathers were faith-based to the core. They saw the formation of this country as a divine calling, and its long-term success would take a people trusting God and being undivided. That calling has never changed.

What does all this have to do with occupying and the killing of America? A lot. Jesus said, "Occupy till I come" (Luke 19:13 KJV). This was not a suggestion. It was an instruction to all believers. But what does occupying really mean? What does it look like? To start with, the epitome of occupying is a military term, meaning to take or hold possession or control of territory. And until Jesus Himself taps us on the shoulder and says, "Come on. Well done, good and faithful servant," we are supposed to be fighting and gaining territory for God.

Numerous times in the Bible, God encouraged His people to go in, take, and occupy the land that He was giving them.

> *Then Caleb silenced the people before Moses, saying, "Let us go up and occupy it, for we are well able to conquer it"* (Numbers 13:30 NET).
>
> *Look! I have already given the land to you. Go,* ***occupy*** *the territory that I, the Lord, promised to give to your ancestors Abraham, Isaac, and Jacob, and to their descendants* (Deuteronomy 1:8 NET).

Other translations of Luke 19:13 read, "Engage in business until I come" (ESV). "Put this money to work…until I come back" (NIV). Jesus was speaking in a parable concerning ten servants who were each given ten minas (about three months' wages) with the responsibility of multiplying them. The clear implication for our purposes in this book is, "I'm coming back. So be ready." But that doesn't mean disengaging and sitting back on your laurels. It means get moving and working while you watch.

Both of our fathers were in the Air Force. One term that Teri's father used repeatedly in child-rearing was something that he used as an officer: "Hustle, hustle, hustle!" The definition of hustle from the American Heritage Dictionary, Fifth Edition is "to move or act energetically and rapidly. To push or force one's way. To act aggressively, especially in business dealings." In other words, move it out in all areas for God.

"Use your talents and finances, whatever I've given you, to multiply and increase your territory." Increasing what God has given us is biblical. Taking what we have and sitting on it is not. Answer this question: How can you prosper and expand territory, which includes your influence and values upon your circle, if your freedoms are being shut down? You can't.

That's why communism and socialism fail. Those opposed to Christianity—including Communists, socialists and Marxists—want to take our territory and reduce our influence. Occupying involves growing and being productive people, building the walls of protection around our expanding territory, monitoring the gates, and guarding our biblically based values that are our constitutional right.

Gene wrote in his previous book "Flashpoint of Revival": "Many Christians are waiting on God to send down revival, but God is waiting on the Church to rise up."

Stop looking for the other guy to do it. God uses masses to create waves, but those masses are made up of individuals. God uses individuals. He's all about the ones. Like a stone being tossed into a lake, quite often it is the one moving in faith who begins the ripple that becomes a wave.

Can we turn this nation around? Absolutely. Is it going to be a battle? You bet. But we have to start. We have to start at the local level, in our neighborhoods, in our local school boards and churches, not afraid to push back and preach the uncompromising truth. We have to vote with our pocketbooks, hitting businesses supporting woke ideology where it hurts most. We can't be lethargic and think our seemingly small part doesn't matter. Without you added to the others being undivided as one entity, the wave never forms.

You, yes you, choosing a local coffee shop over Starbucks, saying "no" to Target and Disney, turning off secular media affecting their ratings, canceling woke companies before they have a chance to cancel you. That's where we have to turn this around.[4]

Let's face it, there is evil in all parties that have either been bought out or intimidated. The time for "auto pilot" thinking is dead and gone. We all need to be fully engaged and alert, a watchman over every area of our lives. Sitting on your sofa flipping the channels with popcorn and soda while America is burning[5] and our kids are being indoctrinated—just occupying space—is not what Jesus meant![6]

Yes, a president is critical, but he or she can't change the culture or the hearts of a culture. That starts with us. Is it going to be a fight? You bet. Are we in the last days? You bet. But Scripture tells us to occupy until He comes, not wait for the next bus. Look, we are already making an impact. We can't wimp out now.

During the process of writing this book, we were consistently seeing updates that we've informed you about. Here's another one. In July 2023, the following report came out. As of August 2023, the movie *Sound of Freedom* (a powerful and sobering faith-based film)[7] has grossed $248 million worldwide.[8] Meanwhile, Disney lost $900-plus million on their last eight releases.[9] Diane Ackerman in an article on Samuel Adams wrote, "Early on, he realized that revolutions don't require a majority to prevail, but rather an irate, tireless minority keen to set brushfires in people's minds."[10]

Let's be the ones setting brushfires of freedom. Like ripples lead to waves, brushfires lead to wildfires! While writing this chapter, horrific wildfires raged through Maui, Hawaii, destroying property and taking lives. We would never rejoice in that kind of physical devastation. However in the spiritual realm, we can see a prophetic wildfire blowing through this nation and burning the evil agendas and spirits behind them. We need a wildfire of sanity to sweep across the land, burning up the lunacy.

BLESS ME INDEED

When thinking of occupying, we'd be remiss if we didn't remember the audacious, faith-filled fellow in the Old Testament named Jabez. He was all about occupying and letting God expand his territory.

> *And Jabez called on the God of Israel saying, "Oh, that You would bless me indeed, and enlarge my territory, that Your hand would be with me, and that You would keep me from evil, that I may not cause pain!" So God granted him what he requested* (1 Chronicles 4:10 NKJV).

What an amazing prayer. And God granted his request! "…ye have not, because ye ask not," declares James 4:2 (KJV). We need to ask God without hesitation to enlarge our territory of influence in the arenas He has appointed us to. Yet we have to ask with the right motives. James 4:3 (NKJV) says, "You ask and do not receive, because you ask amiss, that you may spend it on your pleasures." Jabez received because his motives were honorable. "Now Jabez was more honorable than his brothers" (1 Chronicles 4:9 NKJV).

Nothing is more honorable than asking God to expand our territory to promote godly values and freedom, shut down evil that is being celebrated, protect our children, and preserve America's calling to be a conduit for the Gospel. There's nothing more honorable than Nehemiah's cry, "Do not be afraid of them. Remember the Lord, great and awesome, and fight for your brethren, your sons, your daughters, your wives, and your houses" (Nehemiah 4:14 NKJV). We fight for our circles and territory by occupying with honor.

YES, YOU CAN MAKE A DIFFERENCE

You prove yourself where you are. Bloom where you are planted.

D.L. Moody made it his mission to answer a challenge he heard while just a young shoe salesman: "The world has yet to see what God can do through a man who is fully devoted to Him."[11] He went on to be the most dangerous shoe salesman in Boston—and a revivalist. Time and time again, heaven takes hold of the earnest underdog who is pressing on to be the best he or she can be. Did you know that Joyce Meyer started out as an assistant minister at Life Christian Center, then a storefront church?[12] Smith Wigglesworth was a plumber.

Often, such ones become promoted over those with greater gifting. God sees something in them. They are becoming His word made flesh. They get it into their heart and mind. When that happens, they become explosive. Don't neglect the building up of your mind and inner self.

Now, more than ever, we need leaders who:

1. Are lovers in their quest for Jesus and worship intimately (bridal).
2. Are warriors in their unwavering courage to dismantle the gates of hell (by this I mean they know how to pray).
3. Know how to be statesmen, leaders, and generals discerning what battles to fight. They know when and how to speak! When they speak, they do so with arguments of the Spirit that the enemy cannot stop.

Rick Renner said, "The Bible is full of people…no different than you or I…who heard a word from God, responded in faith, came into divine alignment with what God said, and ultimately saw His word to them fulfilled in their lives. And because of these people's commitment to believe and to possess what God had promised, they changed history!"[13]

I believe as you become true to the voice inside you, you will become the leader God intended you to be at this time in history and accomplish many of the necessary exploits He needs accomplished right now!

EQUIPPED

Most people think they are not equipped enough, that they're not ready. Well, you know what? God birthed you here for this time, this day, at your age, for this moment. He called you. You're here for a reason. There's so many people who are knowledgeable, equipped, and they're sitting in church waiting for somebody to tell them that they're good enough and they're equipped enough.

When I (Gene) think back to my first time in Russia, I came back with an understanding that I had so much of God's word in me that I could have been a bishop of the Christian church in Russia, and I was only 29 years old! My eyes were opened to see that the Russian people had little knowledge of who God is. They didn't understand that He is good. No one had told them that. All they had ever heard was, "God is dead."

So, we have to get off our butts and get moving! The church has been convinced through a lot of reasons, everything from bad pastoring to people who want to control you, that we're not equipped yet. We still believe that we're not good enough, or somehow being a Christian is subclass.

We have to get the mentality that when Jesus went to heaven and put us in charge here on earth until He comes back, He meant, "Act on my behalf. Do what I would do." You are on this planet at this time in H-I-S...S-T-O-R-Y. There is a divine purpose in God's role. It doesn't matter if you're in a wheelchair or if you can't talk. There's something that you can do, that only you can do, for people only you can affect.

You are to be Christ's voice on the earth. Whether you are 3 or 103, you are here for a reason, to help God's kingdom grow and to be a voice in this time. When somebody says, "I don't want to do it," you can be say, "Hey, here I am. Here I am." Be an Isaiah.

> *Then I heard the voice of the Lord saying, "Whom shall I send? And who will go for us?" And I said, "Here am I. Send me!"* (Isaiah 6:8 NIV)

Yes, we are most definitely in the end times. The whole gender identity crisis is another sign because it attacks the very core of creation. Where is there left to go? AI? The end times are accelerating, but some think the end times means we just let it go. But God calls us to occupy. Just because it's the end times doesn't mean we can't have victory. Remember, what the enemy means for evil, the Lord uses for good (see Genesis 50:20)!

Jesus said He's coming back for a glorious church, a beautiful bride, not some worn-out, beat-up spinster. The church needs to prepare for the marriage inside and out and be wedding ready. As T.D. Jakes would say, it's time to "Get ready, get ready, get ready!"

NOTES

1. "Frederick Douglass, 'If there is no struggle, there is no progress,'" *BlackPast,* January 25, 2007; https://www.blackpast

.org/african-american-history/1857-frederick-douglass-if-there-no-struggle-there-no-progress/; accessed April 23, 2024.

2. Frederick Douglass, Narrative of the Life of Frederick Douglass (1845).
3. Patrick Henry, speech, March 4, 1799, quoted in William Wirt Henry, *Patrick Henry: Life, Correspondences and Speeches,* Vol. 2 (1891).
4. "The 10 Most 'Woke' Companies in America," *Newsweek,* August 12, 2022; https://www.pressreader.com/usa/newsweek/20220812/281900186970721; accessed April 23, 2024.
5. "National Fire News," *National Interagency Fire Center,* April 19, 2024; https://www.nifc.gov/fire-information/nfn; accessed April 23, 2024.
6. Douglas Blair, "I'm a Former Teacher. Here's How Your Children Are Getting Indoctrinated by Leftist Ideology," *The Heritage Foundation, August* 17, 2020; https://www.heritage.org/education/commentary/im-former-teacher-heres-how-your-children-are-getting-indoctrinated-leftist; accessed April 23, 2024.
7. *Sound of Freedom,* released by Angel Studios on July 4, 2023; https://www.angel.com/movies/sound-of-freedom; accessed April 23, 2024.
8. Daisy Phillipson, "Sound of Freedom box office: How much has it made?" *Dexerto,* December 27, 2023; https://www.dexerto.com/tv-movies/sound-of-freedom-box-office-how-much-has-it-made-2205789/; accessed April 23, 2024.
9. Paul Sacca, "Staggering Disney box office losses total nearly $900 million for recent movies, according to analysis," *TheBlaze.com;*

https://www.theblaze.com/news/disney-movies-box-office-loses; accessed April 23, 2024.

10. Diane Ackerman, "The Man Who Made a Revolution," *The Daily Resister,* September 2, 2021; http://dailyresister.com/the-man-who-made-a-revolution/; accessed April 23, 2024.
11. Mark Fackler, "The World Has Yet to See...," *Christianity Today;* https://www.christianitytoday.com/history/issues/issue-25/world-has-yet-to-see.html; accessed April 23, 2024.
12. Joyce Meyer Ministries; https://joycemeyer.org/; accessed April 23, 2024.
13. https://www.facebook.com/RickRenner/posts/the-bible-is-full-of-people-no-different-than-you-or-i-who-heard-a-word-from-god/10154275856480964/.

12

THE RED WAVE THAT WAS A RIPPLE

Let's be honest. In 2022 we had rallies. We packed arenas and churches. We were coming out of Covid lockdowns, vaccine mandates that cost many their careers,[1] and even their health,[2] as we've often seen. Many were fed up with what they saw as abuses.

Then there were suspected election integrity issues. Many believe the 2016 presidential elections were heavily compromised. There were many videos and alleged eyewitness reports of possible wrongdoing, and many big-time attorneys were persuaded it was true. With confidence, conservatives were expectant that surely, the "obvious" would be uncovered and revert to the side of freedom and election integrity.

No one wants to lose their freedom, right? So many hoped that what they believed to be gross cheating would be corrected. After all, this is America. The people we trusted were making sure of it. We believed they would do the right thing—that they would certainly have our backs.

Amidst our frustrations, we could sense waves churning under the surface, pressure building against a dam of the "woke" and progressive agendas. We were sure we could see the cracks and fractures in their walls, and with confident hope we were just waiting for them to finally burst. Whenever those walls exploded, there would be an enormous rush of rightfulness flooding through the waterways, channels, conduits, and canals feeding our nation.

Every news outlet, both conservative and liberal, seemed to feel it building. The polls also seemed to indicate the coming pushback was real. Red-blooded, blue-collar, strong-backboned Americans had had enough. Both sides braced themselves for what looked like the inevitable, and the far-left Democrats appeared to be nervous. The backlash of all the evil done was coming. We were finally going to make a strong statement: "You don't mess with America's freedom." God was on our side. This was going to be a massive Red Wave.

But once again, so sure of ourselves, we gleefully reclined in front of our big screens to watch the wave wipe out our opponents. What we got instead was just a ripple. Our victory balloons burst, and our opponents breathed a sigh of relief. The Red Wave was just a facade.

Conservatives were devastated once again. They believed the presidential election was stolen, and this was going to be payback. Meanwhile, the mainstream media had convinced the world that conservatives were anti-freedom. Conservative values were labeled "like semi-fascism"[3]

But the conservative 2016 election cry was simply to "Make America great again." God can raise up whomever He wants, but you have to ask yourself, "Who wouldn't want to make our blessed, God-given nation, the United States of America great again?" We'll tell you who—those who didn't think America was great in the first place and who wanted to basically kill the America we all embrace and love. Frankly, that is the America founded with Judeo-Christian values that believes every life is precious to God and is sickened by abortion and what the Bible calls perversion.

THE RED WAVE RIPPLE

But there was a ripple, and ripples do have effects. Just look what that ripple did. Since Republicans won back the House of Representatives in November 2022 by a razor-thin margin, there has been more accountability and an apparent slowdown of the radical-left agenda.[4] We've seen some of their more prominent leaders removed from the limelight. Investigations of the FBI, the Russian Collusion hoax and some of its major players, along with other significant investigations have come about, all because Republicans won the House. Imagine if there had been a true Red Wave or a spiritual tsunami.

Let's talk about the Dobbs decision, the catalyst that finally overturned the 1973 Roe v. Wade Supreme Court decision that has divided the country over the abortion issue ever since. The landmark decision of 2022, happened as a result of a Supreme Court appointment made during the Trump administration. Who would have thought? Since that fateful day in 1973, the abortion law was so entrenched that many had lost any real hope of it ever being overturned—but nevertheless, Christians continued to fervently pray and take action, and it happened!

I'm sure multitudes of slaves in America more than 100 years ago, had given up hope of ever being free until January 1, 1863, when President Abraham Lincoln issued the Emancipation Proclamation. Though there would be a bloody civil war, nevertheless, the proclamation stood, declaring "that all persons held as slaves are, and henceforward shall be, free."

Multitudes of American slaves had been praying and believing God fervently for generations, longing to be able hear those words. The reality is, however, the Emancipation Proclamation Abraham Lincoln issued on January 1, 1863, didn't really end things for slaves at that time, though the important document declared slaves in the Confederate states (those rebelling against the U.S. government) were free. Because there was no TV or internet, many slaveowners simply kept the information to themselves and didn't tell their slaves. Everything continued as it had been, even though all had changed.

The Southern states continued to hold people in slavery until the end of the Civil War. But when the war ended in May 1865, freeing slaves was enforced by U.S. troops. During the Civil War, there were about 182,566[5] slaves in Texas—most of whom did not know about the Emancipation Proclamation or the ending of the war.

When Major General Gordon Granger arrived in Galveston, Texas, on June 19, 1865, he announced the news of the Emancipation Proclamation in General Order No. 3. To celebrate, Texas began observing June 19 ("Juneteenth") annually, with various festivities such as picnics, barbecues and thanksgiving celebrations. It became a Texas state holiday in 1979 and eventually spread across the nation.

In 2021, it became federal law. Juneteenth is now recognized as a federal holiday. Most Americans don't know this story. Although Juneteenth was not the end of slavery in America, it was an important step in ending it in Texas. The Thirteenth Amendment, passed in January 1865, and was ratified in December of that year, officially ending slavery for the whole nation. Think about that for a minute. It took another two full years after Lincoln's Emancipation Proclamation for the results to be evident in our nation.

Perhaps we need to change our thinking. We're thinking that we have more victories to celebrate in our stand to restore biblical values to America than we know, we just haven't seen the evidence yet. We can't give up. Even with just a red ripple, we are starting to see the beginnings of a tsunami of light.

By using the term "Red Wave," indicating the stand and political gains made by conservative Republican voters, we're not saying being a Democrat is evil. But clearly, the party's current agenda, platform and policies don't match up with biblical values or the agenda of the founders.[6] It seems the Democratic party has been hijacked by the radical far-left, woke agenda. They are far more left than traditional liberals. At least a traditional liberal will engage in dialogue, work together with others of differing points of view, and be willing to meet somewhere in the middle. A traditional liberal is for traditional America.

Although the Red Wave did not manifest as much as we had hoped, the red ripple did have some impact. Races were won and elections were tighter than the Left thought they would be. It seemed to make them sweat a little and to many of them, it may have been a clear rebuke to their overconfidence.

Yes conservative Republicans won the House only by a slight margin, but we did win, and we have seen some progress. Can you imagine if the Democrats had won both the House and Senate? It could have been a final dose of lethal poison for our Lady Liberty. The narrow margin of conservative Republican victory further affirmed how divided our nation really is.

To test this statement, just go to any public university and shout, "America is great!" and see what happens. People ask, "How could you vote for some of those right-wing Republican candidates? One of them, especially, seems so arrogant and rude." Really? Sometimes arrogant and rude is misconstrued boldness and confidence that we really need in a strong leader who will resolutely stand firm and not back down to opposition.

We recommend whether Democrat, Republican or Independent, you vote the values that this country was founded on and cast your ballot in line with the Mayflower Compact and U.S. Constitution.

LEFT FOR DEAD

In the Bible, in Acts 14, there is an account of what happened to a strong and confident leader named Paul. He stood up and boldly proclaimed the good news of the Gospel of Jesus Christ in the city of Lystra in modern-day Turkey. Some leaders from the previous city where Paul had preached and who had strongly opposed his message, making plans to kill him there, had followed him to Lystra. There they stirred up the people of Lystra to kill Paul. A mob began throwing rocks and ultimately stoned Paul.

They dragged him outside the city and left him for dead. But Paul wasn't dead, only nearly dead. God raised up the apostle as his friends stood around him and prayed, and then powerfully moved through him to establish the Church of the Lord Jesus Christ throughout the known world at that time.

Just as the apostle Paul was left for dead centuries ago, those intent on killing America believe that she is dead. Many who will read these words believe she is as good as dead, and that it's only a matter of time before our freedoms will be finally snuffed out. We can feel your sighs. We can hear you saying:

> I'd love to believe everything you've written, Gene and Teri, but we're "hoped out." The Bible says, in Proverbs 13:12 (NKJV) that "Hope deferred makes the heart sick." Our hope has been deferred again and again. We're heartsick and disillusioned. Covid hit, and it seems to us that it was used as a weapon to shut everyone down and control us. We prayed, but all we saw was the elections going south, way south. We believe the elections were stolen, even though we prayed.
>
> So, we ask ourselves, can and will we ever have an honest election again? America seems to have lost

> its innocence and lost its way. We are starting to understand just how deep some of the bad stuff goes. Now we suspect everyone and everything. If you can control the media and what people think, then you can take over elections. That's what we think happened.
>
> We seem to have lost our voices. Even the safe places we trusted for accurate information have turned their backs on us. They even canceled Tucker Carlson! We used to watch the news—conservative news—and get fired up. But now we mostly tune out because what we hear sounds to us like just a bunch of controlled lies.
>
> We're weary, Gene and Teri, just tired. We hear you talking about hope. But why is it taking so long? Surely the corruption and evil can't get much worse!

We hear you, and we understand. But God still has a plan. The Holy Spirit of God's remnant of people with strong biblical values is still inside America, and she will be raised. We were expecting a huge wave, and when it didn't happen, we became disillusioned. But it was our own fault.

WHAT HAPPENED AND WHY

The biggest issue with the Red Wave that ended up being a ripple, wasn't what did or didn't happen in that specific election. It was that we were expecting a quick fix that would solve all our problems instead of working to fix them. That's where we fail, if there is a failure.

It may have been that we weren't paying enough attention, maybe not working hard enough or taking the time to adequately prepare. We may have also underestimated the magnitude of what we were up against and failed to be as strategic and persistent as the opposition. But we also believe that a big reason may have been that the election could have been corrupted. From that point of view, we may indeed have had a Red Wave, but not the way we thought it was going to be.

Maybe, if enough of us conservatives would have engaged, we could at least interrupted, if not severely hampered, the tsunami of opposition against biblical values. But the truth is, the slide away from those values has been going on for decades in our political, educational and governmental systems. We are now more open to understanding the importance of school boards, city councils and the power of municipal elections. Up until this point, however, most people could care less about who was on their school boards, city councils or within the bureaucratic hierarchy of their local governments.

Now, we want to know because we don't want our children and grandchildren being negatively influenced by the left-wing agenda. We want them to learn good ol' reading, writing, and arithmetic, and we're taking our stand, and winning! Case in point:

In the Madison Public Library in Huntsville, Alabama, a Brave Books reading event for kids with Kirk Cameron was canceled for "safety occupancy" reasons, while transvestite or cross-dresser story hours were still fine. An article in *Movieguide,* a family guide to movies and entertainment, reported:

> Given Brave Books' conservative and Christian values, however, the event organizers felt that the cancelation of the event was fueled by political bias more than anything else.
>
> "Upon learning that Mr. Cameron and his friend and Brave Books author, Riley Gaines, will be attending in person, you abruptly canceled the event citing 'security concerns' from a potential protest of Mr. Cameron and claiming the event exceeds the library's capacity," Cameron and Brave Books' legal counsel Jeremy Dys said in response to the library's statement.
>
> "As a recipient of federal funds, the ALA is prohibited from using taxpayer dollars to violate the First Amendment," Dys further explained. "The senators also make clear that religious groups and organizers deserve equal treatment under the law."
>
> Cameron not only refused to let the library take away his First Amendment right but also believes the "See You at the Library Day" will benefit struggling libraries nationwide.
>
> "These libraries should really be grateful that so many parents and children are excited to visit them tomorrow," Cameron told CBN's *Faithwire.* "With e-books and other online reading options, sit-down libraries are becoming irrelevant and obsolete to the younger generation."

> "Too much fear and woke-ness has made the ALA and these librarians go mad," he continued.[7]

The good news is the Madison Public Library reversed its decision after the backlash from Cameron and Brave Books! Kirk Cameron and Brave Books are definitely "gatekeepers" of biblical values and the right for them to be heard.

You don't have to be famous to be a gatekeeper.

Parents in Montgomery County, Maryland, challenged their local school board on teaching children as young as kindergarten from inclusive LGBTQIA+ books. The county's schools had given parents no way to opt out, so concerned parents linked arms and pushed back. In August 2023, they lost their initial case in a federal court to be granted a preliminary injunction to immediately opt their kids out of engaging with the books. A 2-1 decision in a federal court ruled against the families. The county schools' statement said: "MCPS [Montgomery County Public Schools] expects all classrooms to be inclusive and safe spaces for students, including those who identify as LGBTQ+ community.... Students and families may not choose to opt out of engaging with any instructional materials, other than "Family Life and Human Sexuality Unit of Instruction" which is specifically permitted by Maryland law. As such, teachers will not send home letters to inform families when inclusive books are read in the future."[8]

Though an apparent loss, the lawsuit drew national attention and will likely inspire others to stand up, and speak up, in their own school districts.

☆ ☆

It's no secret that in recent decades, our culture has fallen to the lowest of tides away from the secure moorings of biblical values and the beliefs of our founders. Yet it's at the lowest of tides that a tsunami of light can arise. When things look the darkest, just one person upholding the light can dissipate that darkness. You, our friend, are that light.

Our deepest desire is that you now see that your light shining in darkness is key. In the absence of holding up your light, a tsunami of darkness can remain unchallenged and flood into every crevice and corner. Commit to doing everything you can to shed the light of biblical values and righteousness into every corner of our nation. When all hold their candles of light, we can challenge any darkness with a tsunami of light that can have profound influence on future generations.

You have never been more valuable and needed as now!

NOTES

1. Andrea Hsu, "Thousands of Workers Are Opting to Get Fired Rather Than Take the Vaccine," *NPR,* October 24, 2021; https://www.npr.org/2021/10/24/1047947268/covid-vaccine-workers-quitting-getting-fired-mandates# and Amanda del Castillo, "COVID vaccine refusal 10th highest reason for job cuts in 2021, report says," *ABC7News,* Bay Area, November 5, 2021; https://abc7news.com/jan-4-vaccine-mandate-biden-nationwide-january-4th/11200414/; both accessed April 23, 2024.

2. T. Jefferson, "Public should be told that vaccines may have long term adverse effects," *National Library of Medicine,* January 16, 1999; https://www.ncbi.nlm.nih.gov/pmc/articles/PMC1114674/.

3. Rebecca Shabad, "Biden blasts MAGA philosophy as 'semi-fascism,'" *NBC,* August 26, 2022; https://www.nbcnews.com/politics/2022-election/biden-blasts-maga-philosophy-semi-fascism-rcna44953; accessed April 23, 2024.

4. John F. Harris, "The Left Goes to War With Itself," *Politico Magazine,* Altitude, June 23, 2022; https://www.politico.com/news/magazine/2022/06/23/the-new-battles-roiling-the-left-00041627; accessed April 23, 2024.

5. "The African-American Story," *Texas State History Museum,* https://www.thestoryoftexas.com/discover/campfire-stories/african-americans; accessed April 23, 2024.

6. "Party Platform," *The Democratic Platform,* democrats.org, https://democrats.org/where-we-stand/party-platform/; accessed April 23, 2024.

7. "Alabama Library Backtracks After Attempt to Cancel Kirk Cameron Event," *Movieguide,* August 10, 2023; ahttps://www.movieguide.org/news-articles/library-backtracks-after-attempt-to-cancel-kirk-cameron-event.html; accessed April 23, 2024.

8. Ida Domingo, "Montgomery County Parents to Challenge School Board over LGBTQ+ Curriculum Policy in Court," *ABC7 News,* August 9, 2023; https://wjla.com/news/crisis-in-the-classrooms/montgomery-county-mahmoud-mcknight-oral-arguments-religious-parents-lawsuit-opt-out-option-lgbtq-curriculum-policy-schools-mcps-books-reading-materials-classroom-gay-queer-maryland-dmv-education; accessed April 23, 2024.

13

A TSUNAMI OF LIGHT

Were the founding fathers prophetic? The way they saw into the future and framed the Constitution for our protection, you would think God's Spirit was on them. The same with President Ronald Reagan when he said:

> Freedom is never more than one generation away from extinction. We didn't pass it on to our children in the bloodstream. The only way they can inherit the freedom we have known is if we fight for it, protect it, defend it, and then hand it to them with the well fought lessons of how they in their lifetime must do the same. And if you and I don't do this, then you and I may well spend our sunset years telling our children and our children's children what it once was like in America when men were free.[1]

Someone wise added, "If you leave your children or grandchildren a world where you never stood up, they'll inherit a world where they can't." The question is, what are we going to do? The choice is ours. We say "ours" because it is going to take all of us pulling together as one, even if we disagree on some things. We're going to have to fight for it alongside people we don't totally agree with, maybe even the ones sitting next to us at church.

We're not saying you should agree with heresy or follow unbiblical and ungodly teaching, but we have to be willing to see things differently, including each other. God has designed us to need each other, and none of us can do this all alone.

Are we going to collectively draw that line in the sand and say, "Enough is enough" and then stand firm? Are we going to lay fear aside and step forward when the call comes to us personally?

"Fear is a reaction," said Winston Churchill, "Courage is a decision." Now is not the time to cower in fear but to make the decision to be courageous. What are we going to do? What are we going to leave to our children and grandchildren and the next generation? This is bigger than Gene and Teri, bigger than you.

No doubt, many voices from the opposition are screaming things we should be concerned about, things that want to make us overcome with fear. Yet we are in a time when, as Robert Louis Stevenson said, "Keep your fears to yourself but share your courage with others." The time has come for courage and pulling together.

Throughout this book we have alluded to the tsunami of darkness that has hit our nation. When a tsunami occurs, there's a shift in the earth's crust miles below the ocean's surface. It's a destructive, harmful event because of a planet broken by sin's curse until God's legal plan to deal with satan comes to completion and God restores the earth.

Paul said, "We know that the whole creation has been groaning as in the pains of childbirth right up to the present time" (Romans 8:22 NIV). One commentator wrote, "Not only does creation groan in its fallen state for future redemption (8:22), but *Christians* also groan for that day as well (8:23). ...There is *no* aspect of creation that is free from the pain of the consequence of sin."[2]

A physical tsunami is the earth groaning in pain because of its brokenness. As the shift in the plates occurs, it causes the ground to buckle, which causes the water sitting on top of it to vibrate and move. Whatever the depth of the water is, it begins to propagate out in every direction.

As the tsunami advances toward shore, the ocean gets shallower and shallower as the water is sucked back into the tide, increasing its size and power. Eventually, the column of water stands up as high as 100 feet, and it continues to stand up as long as it's rolling in.

A tsunami can carry the power of millions of megatons of TNT. With a wave height of 127 feet, the 2011 tsunami in Japan released some 9,320,000 megatons of TNT energy. That's more powerful than the nuclear explosion at Hiroshima.[3] When it hits the land, the water is like a hammer at 8.34 pounds per gallon. So if a home or building gets hit with just 100,000 gallons, which is only about one-third the size of an Olympic swimming pool, it's getting crushed with 834,000 pounds. That's a lot of punch.

Multiply that a hundred miles wide and the water hammer smashes everything in its path and continues until there's enough resistance or it's going uphill and eventually dies down.

We saw this parallel happening in American culture. Spiritually, there was a shift in the plates of worldview happening under the surface. The first ripple waves began building up and eventually became a tsunami wave that made a deep impact, changing the foundational landscape of our belief system. This is why we're seeing the unusual things we've been seeing.

With a crushed foundational belief system, people have been shaken to the core. Family structures have crumbled. Identities have crumbled. Purpose for living has crumbled. People wonder who they are. Men can have babies[4] and professors can't determine male from female.[5] A baby inside the womb can be aborted, but if it's born premature it's put on life support. Crazy.

What's real and what's not real? What is truth? Most believe truth is relative—whatever you want. And if you disagree, instead of engaging in a healthy debate you can get labeled everything from a Christian Nationalist to a racist, bigot, supremacist, domestic terrorist, or whatever the newest derogatory descriptor is. This is all because of a radical breakdown in values that directly affects America.

In the physical, before the tsunami hits land, as the tide is receding, everything appears peaceful and calm except for the exceptionally shallow water and the sand crabs scurrying, sea gulls hunkering down, nature sensing something happening in the environment. Discerning people who know the signs also understand what is about to take place. Even though there is apparent peace, the impact of destruction is soon to hit. Some get away to higher ground, taking family and friends with them, and are saved. Others, however, are so caught up in the tranquil beauty of their surroundings that they can't grasp what is about to occur.

In America, the sand crabs and seagulls and discerning people have been warning us for years that something big was about to hit. Many could see it coming, even prophetically warned the nation. Yet most couldn't wrap their minds around the destruction and depravity that has become a reality—not here, not in America.[6] We had no idea how deep the corruption and evil ideology was.[7] But it's here. The tsunami has hit and the damage is significant. For example, how many lives were lost during Covid that could have been prevented with the administering of cheaper treatments, like Ivermectin and hydroxychloroquine.

> According to a new peer-reviewed ecological study, a natural experiment occurred when the government of Peru authorized ivermectin for use during the COVID-19 pandemic resulting in evidence of the drug's effectiveness and ability to reduce excess deaths. The paper's results, published August 8 [2023] in Cureus, found a 74 percent reduction in excess deaths in 10 states with the most intensive ivermectin use over a 30-day period following peak deaths during the pandemic...When ivermectin was available without restriction, there was a fourteenfold reduction in nationwide excess deaths. Once access to ivermectin was restricted by the government, a thirteenfold increase in excess deaths

> was observed in the two months following the limitation of its use.[8]

How many people did not have to die? And why? It's ludicrous to believe they did not know the effectiveness of these other treatments. In our opinion, it's criminal and almost like it was planned. How many lives, particularly young children and teens, have been damaged beyond repair by the transgender[9] and the LGBTQIA+ tidal wave that has pushed violently through our schools?[10] "Why do drag queens insist on performing in elementary schools in front of young children when they have places to perform in front of adults? Why do the schools allow them to?"[11]

We believe it's because they have an agenda—our children. We wonder how many souls have been lost because of the war against anything biblical or godly? Yes, it appears to us that the tsunami of darkness has hit.

NOW, THE REALLY GOOD NEWS

Believe it or not, there is good news amid the devastation—really good news. The tsunami that was intended to drown America, to kill her, has not reached up to Lady Liberty's head. She is still breathing. Interestingly, tsunamis come in a series of tidal waves known as the tsunami wave train. The initial waves have hit the American culture and caused significant damage, but the following waves haven't hit yet, and we can slow them drastically and even stop them completely! America can rise out of the chaos and be stronger than ever.

A TRUE TSUNAMI MIRACLE

When talking about tsunamis, we can't forget Sunday morning, December 26, 2004. On that fateful day, Indonesia experienced the deadliest tsunami in known history, taking the lives of more than 230,000 people across 14 countries. It began at 7:59 a.m. local time, when a 9.1-magnitude quake struck off the northern tip of Sumatra.[12]

That day, Pastor Dayalan Sanders[13] of Sri Lanka was preparing for his sermon, walking the beach near his home and orphanage. He and his wife, Kokila, had a three-year-old daughter and cared for 28 orphans. As Dayalan strolled along the beach, he heard what sounded like a thousand freight trains in the distance.

When he looked up, he saw the Goliath tidal wave rushing toward them. Their small beachside orphanage was directly in the path of a massive tidal wave. A 30-foot-high wall of water stretching from one end of the beach to the other was charging toward them.

Dayalan's wife was in the kitchen with their daughter. With only seconds to spare, he yelled at the top of his lungs and ordered everyone at the orphanage to run to a boat that was afloat on the side of the house. When he helped everyone into the boat, he then asked for his daughter and gripped her like a vice in his arms. Thirty-two people, including the boat's driver, who was a personal friend, were crammed in the 15-foot boat with a small 15-horsepower engine. It could barely tow the weight of them all.

As the massive wall of ocean water continued to gain strength, something miraculous had to happen if they were going to make it out alive. This was it. Faced with certain death, in that moment the Scripture verse Isaiah 59:29 popped into Dayalan's mind. He stood with his hand out and proclaimed, "Based on the strength of the Scriptures, when it says the enemy comes in like a flood, the Spirit of the Lord shall raise up a standard against it. I command you in the name of Jesus. Stop!"

What happened next was an authentic miracle. The wall of water that was seconds away from hammering into them suddenly dropped down and began straining against what seemed like an invisible wall. The tide was laboring to break free, but something was holding it back.

"The only force of power that would've stopped it," said Dayalan, "was the power of God. And God, with his power and with his hand, slowed down and stopped the wave for us and gave us time to get away."

Before they could get away, however, they had to get the boat started. It cranked on the first pull! According to Dayalan, that was another miracle because it normally took three or four pulls before it started. The boat with 32 passengers hanging on for dear life managed to escape the first wave, yet their ordeal was far from over. While puttering full throttle to get away, a second wave was rapidly bearing down on them, threatening to swallow them from behind.

It was during the second wave that Dayalan ordered his friend driving the boat to turn around and head straight into the oncoming wave. An experienced fisherman, the driver told Dayalan that attacking the wave head on was extremely dangerous and not a good idea. "I thought we were all going to die that day," he said. But Dayalan had made up his mind. "You do what I tell you to do," he ordered. "Turn north first, and we are going to take this head-on!"

And so the small fiberglass boat went full throttle into the wave. "When we hit the bottom of the wave it kept pushing us back, and we were restraining it in the name of Jesus. And then the hand of God lifted the boat, and he placed us right on top of the wave."

An hour later, the whole thing was over. By the hand of God, Dayalan Sanders, his family, friend, and 28 children had survived the deadly tsunami. But the orphanage he took 20 years to build was destroyed in a matter of seconds.

"Tsunamis could take anything and everything from us," said Dayalan, "but the word of God, it never can because it's more powerful than anything in this whole world." Dayalan said he was determined to rebuild and felt strongly that this was where God wanted him to be and where God wanted him to witness for him, and all the children there one day would be powerfully used by God. Dayalan Sanders did rebuild, and his ministry and orphanage is thriving to this day.

A TSUNAMI OF LIGHT

Sometimes it takes a tsunami to stop a tsunami. That wall of ocean lost its power against the light of God's word. There's another shift happening below the surface of the culture. It's stirring and creating another type of tsunami, a tsunami of light—light shining on all the darkness. People are seeing the truth and waking up. Media ratings have shifted massively. American's trust in media has hit an all-time low, which is an indication of the mindset of Americans.[14]

Our *Flashpoint Live* has exploded with viewers, and a flood of people are calling daily concerned about the state of America. The saying, "Go woke, go broke," is certainly proving true.[15] Sex trafficking and out-of-control crime is at the forefront of people's minds. People see these realities and are fed up. Light exposes the darkness, and we are seeing an exposure of demonic agendas revealed for all the world to see. We're seeing a wave of spiritual awakening, even on college campuses. There is a shift of light shining in the darkness.

"All the darkness can't extinguish the light of a single candle," said Francis of Assisi. "The light shines in the darkness, and the darkness has not overcome it" (John 1:5 NIV). If one candle can dispel the darkness in an entire room, think what an army of candles can do.

There will always be darkness. We will always be in a war. This thing is ongoing. But to sit back and not occupy is not God's way. We have a choice to turn back the tide just like Pastor Dayalan Sanders did. "When the enemy comes in, like a flood the Spirit of the Lord will lift up a standard against him" (Isaiah 59:19 NKJV).

What is that standard? It is the Spirit of the Lord, and it is His people who have the Spirit of the Lord inside them. "We are not to simply bandage the wounds of victims beneath the wheels of injustice," wrote Deitrich Bonhoeffer, "we are to drive a spoke into the wheel itself."[16]

We have an opportunity, not to bandage our wounds, but to drive a stake in the wheel. Darkness will always be among us, but light dispels the darkness. Be a vessel of light. "You are the light of the world. A city that is set on a hill cannot be hidden" (Matthew 5:14 NKJV).

THREE STEPS TO LIBERTY

1. WE MUST CONTINUE TO PRAY AND SEEK GOD'S FACE.

We must speak to the tsunami with the word of God and a spiritual wall will rise up. The enemy wants us to not pray. The flesh wants to tell us that prayer doesn't work. But Jesus told us to always pray and not lose heart (see Luke 18:1). This means prayer takes persistence. In the book of Colossians, the apostle Paul tells the believers that Epaphras is "always wrestling in prayer for you, that you may stand firm in all the will of God" (Colossians 4:12 NIV).

Prayer is wrestling. Prayer with a shovel works. It's more than asking God for stuff. It's spiritual warfare.

> *For we do not wrestle against flesh and blood, but against principalities, against powers, against the rulers of the darkness of this age, against spiritual hosts of wickedness in the heavenly places* (Ephesians 6:12 NKJV).

Second Chronicles 7:14 (NKJV) has been a rallying call to prayer for decades. It. Still. Is. When you break down this prayer into practical elements it gives us a biblical strategy:

- "If My people who are called by My name"—God's people. Not the world. Believers who know Him. It starts with us.
- "will humble themselves"—We have to get real about ourselves and not be pious and safe in our church buildings.
- "and pray and seek My face"—Are we really seeking God's face and direction or are we just talking about politics and asking Him to bless our efforts?
- "and turn from their wicked ways"—God is calling us to holiness. Us before them. We can't preach it if we are not living it.
- "then I will hear from heaven, and will forgive their sin"—God, forgive us first.
- "and heal their land"—Yes, we are in the end times, but God still wants to heal our land. Remember, we are to occupy until He comes.

"For he spoke and stirred up a tempest that lifted high the waves" (Psalm 107:25 NIV). God is in control of the waves.

2. TURN OUR BOATS AROUND AND HEAD STRAIGHT INTO THE TSUNAMI.

That's our call too! We must charge into the waves of opposition like David charged Goliath. We can't be timid and afraid of it, but must advance full throttle. Whether it is spiritual, political, economic, or emotional, the wave can take you to where you want to go or it can leave you devastated, out of control, and defeated. Again, the choice is yours. Our friend Tim Sheets prophesied:[17]

> It will be an effortless motion as you are swiftly pulled up on top of the waves, but it will require surrender.... Strongholds that we have spent years praying into to break, will be flattened in a moment in this coming hour. You will ride high atop the waves of awakening and revival, and you do not need to fear the incoming waves. It is going to be a wild ride of excitement, so stand still, watch the horizon and brace for what is about to come. The countless numbers of people that I saw, I believe, represent the prodigal that will return to the Father in this hour's awakening. They will be swept up in this mighty movement and will be carried upon the rivers of His living water. God is moving mightily, the ground is ready and prepared, the

harvest is ripe. Continue standing guard, continue standing on the Word, continue worshipping and watch as the Lord springs up ancient wells within you, as He exposes wickedness to run in fear, and causes a mighty outpouring of His Spirit, cleansing and refreshing to pour out across the tired and weary earth. Begin calling in the waves, begin calling in the lost in your family who will be swept up in this wave (not drowned by it, but carried upon it.) Keep speaking to the mountains of impossibility—they are about to be flattened before you. The Waymaker is on the move. Position yourself in readiness.

3. REBUILD STRONGER.

Pastor Dayalan said he was determined to rebuild stronger because God had called him to that place. We are called to a place. America. This is our home. This is our Ziklag. After tsunamis, earthquakes, and hurricanes, engineers build structures more impenetrable to future catastrophes. They look at the engineering aspect of it and analyze what went wrong, and they build it back better so that it can withstand storms.

After hurricane Katrina, in New Orleans they reworked the levee system. That's their land. And there's a group of people there who are not leaving. They learned how to build the cemeteries and everything else; they are not leaving. They are possessing their land and standing there and learning how to build it so they can withstand storms in the future. They are occupying. They can maintain their territory and will not be intimidated.

When we think of a tsunami, we think death and destruction, but I want us to think of a move of God so powerful that it literally reshapes the landscape. To stop the killing of America it is going to take power—the power of God to change the landscape. You can always see where a tsunami hit land because the fruit is evident.

Perhaps one of the most important positive effects of tsunamis is a redistribution of nutrients. Tsunami waves can lift up nutrient-rich sediment in estuaries and deltas and disperse it inland. In so doing, tsunamis help to spread nutrients in agricultural areas, thus increasing the fertility of the soil. In the same vein, tsunamis can also create new habitats. We can stop the insanity by changing the landscape.

A PROPHETIC WORD ABOUT REBUILDING

In the establishment of this country, there were documents set in place by our founding fathers that are now being ignored, such as the Constitution.[18] We were not established to be ruled over by the government. Our country was established on God-centered principles, and we were born with certain inalienable rights.

It is time to rebuild America based on the founding fathers' pillars of faith. It is time to rebuild with the reinforcement that we were made in the image of God, for a divine purpose, and have definite identities. We are individuals, not a collective. We need to rebuild our acknowledgment that we are not our own gods. Everyone does not have their own reality.

We need to rebuild on truth because the truth will set you free. We need to rebuild ensuring we are working toward a free country—not toward a world-centered, tyrannical, elitist-run, greater-good world order. God will defend His nation. He will give us new strategies. It is our opinion that God will bring a radical change to our nation.

Many have prophesied this country will not go under but stand stronger than ever. Kenneth Copeland, Hank Kunnemann, Dutch Sheets, Tim Sheets, Kent Christmas, Robin Bullock. We will have revival, reformation, and a return to God like never before.

In our opinion, when we compare evil—the attempted chaos, sexual perversion, division, tyranny, corrupt finances—versus good, there's one choice that is obvious. "Hell doesn't have a chance against our God," Tim Sheets said. "This tsunami is clearing out the filth of evil…Don't listen to known liars."[18]

Justice is coming. It's been slow in coming, but it is starting to trickle in. We're expecting a tsunami of justice very soon. That ought to help you discern whom you should not listen to. We repeat, do not listen to known liars. Yes, there's a shaking going down, but God and His kingdom is rising up. We strongly suggest you join the winning team.

Since we started this chapter with a Ronald Reagan quote, it seems appropriate to conclude with one. President Regan said:

> To all those trapped in tyranny, wherever they may be, let us speak with one voice—not as Republicans or Democrats, but as Americans—saying you are not alone; your dreams are not in vain. Hold on to your dreams, because the tide of the future is a freedom tide, and totalitarianism cannot hold it back.[19]

There is a tide of light, of God and liberty, that is pushing back the darkness. It's not just a wave or a ripple, but a tsunami that can't be held back. America was founded on godly principles. We've seen that as a fact. And they are not killing her. We won't let that happen. We are turning back the tsunami of darkness and Lady Liberty is rising!

NOTES

1. Ronald Reagan, speech, Phoenix Chamber of Commerce, March 30, 1961.
2. Grant, "Romans 8:22," *Verse by Verse Commentary,* December 8, 2012, https://versebyversecommentary.com/2012/12/08/romans-822; accessed April 23, 2024.
3. Brian Wang, "Nuclear tsunami would have less energy and die out before getting far inland," *Next Big Future,* April 24, 2018; https://www.nextbigfuture.com/2018/04/nuclear-tsunami-would-have-less-energy-and-die-out-before-getting-far-inland.html; accessed April 23, 2024.
4. Julie Compton, "Trans dads tell doctors: 'You can be a man and have a baby,'" *NBC News,* May 19, 2019; https://www.nbcnews

.com/feature/nbc-out/trans-dads-tell-doctors-you-can-be-man-have-baby-n1006906; accessed April 23, 2024.

5. Natalie O'Neill, "'Woke' University of Pittsburgh professor denies difference in male, female skeletons," *New York Post,* March 31, 2023; https://nypost.com/2023/03/31/woke-professor-denies-male-female-skeleton-differences/; accessed April 23, 2024.

6. Madeline Crabb, "Depravity, delusion, and destruction—Signs of post-Christian America," *Renew America,* May 30, 2015; http://renewamerica.com/columns/crabb/150530; accessed April 23, 2024.

7. Calley Griffin and Amy Mackinnon, "Report: Corruption in U.S. at Worst Levels in Almost a Decade," *Foreign Policy,* January 28, 2021; https://foreignpolicy.com/2021/01/28/report-transparency-international-corruption-worst-decade-united-states/; accessed April 23, 2024.

8. Megan Redshaw, "Intensive Ivermectin Use Had 74 Percent Reduction in Excess Deaths in Peru: New Study," *The Epoch Times,* August 17, 2023, https://www.theepochtimes.com/mkt_app/health/most-intensive-ivermectin-use-had-74-percent-reduction-in-excess-deaths-in-peru-new-study-5470885; accessed April 23, 2024.

9. "Detransitioners: What Is It Like to Be One?" *DTS,* https://detransitionsurgery.com/detransitioners-experiences-stories/; accessed April 23, 2024.

10. Laura Bult, "Why US schools are at the center of trans rights," *VOX.com,* July 27, 2022; https://www.vox.com/2022/7/27/23279760/trans-rights-school-boards-federal-law; accessed April 23, 2024.

11. Roseanne Colletti, "Elementary Kids Get 'Special Surprise' Drag Performance at School Talent Show," *NBCNewYork,* June 9, 2029; https://www.nbcnewyork.com/news/local/nyc-elementary-kids-get-surprise-drag-queen-performance-talent-show/1700057/; accessed April 23, 2024.

12. "This day in history, December 26, 2004," *History.com;* https://www.history.com/this-day-in-history/tsunami-devastates-indian-ocean-coast; accessed April 23, 2024.

13. "Founder of Orphanage 'Commands' Tsunami to Stop," *Sun Sentinel,* September 27, 2021; https://www.sun-sentinel.com/2004/12/30/founder-of-orphanage-commands-tsunami-to-stop-saves-28-children/; accessed April 23, 2024.

14. Sara Fischer, "Americans' trust in media plummets to historic low: poll," *AXIOS,* October 24, 2023; https://www.axios.com/2023/10/24/americans-trust-in-media-plummets-to-historic-low-poll; accessed April 23, 2024.

15. Stephen Battaglio, "A wild year for cable news: Shakeups, firings and ratings challenges," *Los Angeles Times,* December 22, 2023; https://www.latimes.com/entertainment-arts/business/story/2023-12-22/a-wild-year-for-cable-news-shakeups-firings-and-falling-ratings-fox-news-cnn-msnb; accessed April 23, 2024.

16. Dietrich Bonhoeffer quote; https://www.goodreads.com/quotes/22884-we-are-not-to-simply-bandage-the-wounds-of-victims; accessed April 23, 2024.

17. Tim Sheets, "The Holy Spirit Tsunami is Here!" Destiny Image, September 13; https://www.destinyimage.com/blog/tim-sheets-the-holy-spirit-tsunami-is-here; accessed April 23, 2024.

18. "Constitution of the United States," U.S. Constitution.congress.gov; https://constitution.congress.gov/constitution/; accessed April 23, 2024.

19. Ronald Reagan, "Remarks on Signing the Captive Nations Week Proclamation," *The American Presidency Project,* July 16, 1984; https://www.presidency.ucsb.edu/documents/remarks-signing-the-captive-nations-week-proclamation; accessed April 23, 2024.

14

BE A HUMAN TSUNAMI

Throughout the history of the United States of America, and the world for that matter, nations and cultures have been impacted by the actions of individuals who weren't afraid to take stands and let their voices be heard. It's mind-boggling the amount of power and influence one person can wield, even when they are seemingly ordinary Joes. They are ordinary, but anything but average.

Jesus used 12 ragtag, uneducated social misfits to move through them to build His church. After the resurrection and the disciples were empowered by the Holy Spirit, they literally turned the world upside down. Once, when Paul and Silas went into a city, the leaders cried out, "These who have turned the world upside down have come here too" (Acts 17:6 NKJV).

Through the Holy Spirit, the disciples and apostles were most definitely human tsunamis. Whatever our world is and our circle of influence, God wants us to turn it upside down. Sometimes, though, a soft word and a whisper can have more power than a shout. At other times, we need to shout. We need to be sensitive to the leading of the Holy Spirit.

When considering human tsunamis, our minds immediately go to the destruction and damage individuals caused. Hitler, charismatic and inspired by evil principalities and powers, amassed a massive wave of followers, creating a tsunami that nearly wiped out Europe and all Jews. Hitler was certain he would rule the world. Little did he know, another tsunami was rising. America and her allies.

Like we've said, sometimes it takes a tsunami to stop a tsunami. Time doesn't allow me to write of Marx, Lenin, Stalin, Mussolini, Pol Pot, Mao Zedong, all destructive tsunamis. Some American leaders have taken our country to death's door.

Yet God uses people. It's amazing what He can do with one person and their gifts. He raises leaders and influencers. There have been powerful tsunamis for the positive. "We must be ready to allow ourselves to be interrupted by God," said Bonhoeffer, "Action springs not from thought, but from a readiness for responsibility." When we do this, it's unlimited what God can do through us for good.

WHAT A GIRL CAN DO

Take Joan of Arc as an awe-inspiring example for all of us of what one person can do. She was most definitely a human tsunami. Though a common medieval peasant girl on the outside, deep inside her core there was a tsunami waiting to be unleashed.

When it was, the world would never be the same. Joan would become a mighty military warrior, something that was unheard of from women in that era. Who would have thought that God would use a simple farmer's daughter to lead a brigade of the French royal army into battle to begin freeing their nation? But then again, that's how God works. He delights in taking ordinary people and using them to impact nations. Joan had some elements inside her—the Spirit of God, love, and a cause bigger than herself.

By the late 1420s, during the Middle Ages, France had been at war with England in what is known as the Hundred Years' War. The kings of England and France had been in conflict with each other for decades and, as is usually the case in war, the common citizens in the country where the fighting took place became innocent victims.

It so happened that most of the warfare occurred on France's home turf. Many peasant farms and villages were decimated by raiding armies, causing untold suffering among the people. At the time Joan of Arc stepped onto the scene, England had been enforcing their will for years, and France's military was depleted and demoralized.

Distraught over the devastation happening to her people, Joan knew something had to be done. Someone had to step up and inspire the troops. But who? A mighty knight? A magnificent warrior? Maybe the king himself?

Yet Joan served an extraordinary God and had an extraordinary relationship with Him. God had been speaking to Joan for a while. As the plight of her country worsened, the intensity of her prayers increased. God answered her cries by giving her a vision and an assignment.

The city of Orleans had been under siege for months and Joan felt part of her divine assignment was to rally a group of soldiers from the royal army and lead them into battle to free the city. Pretty crazy, right? I mean, she was a farm girl in a wool tunic and pigtails. She had no military training, zero, zilch, none. On top of that, how would she convince the king to release a brigade of soldiers to her for this outlandish mission? How would she even get in to see him? She was a low-class nobody, a commoner.

Yeah, the whole idea was insane—or was it? Still, Joan believed God had spoken to her, so she took action, expecting Him to do the unthinkable, the supernatural! I know all of this sounds like a fictional movie for the big screen, but it is a historical reality.

Though she had never laid eyes on the king before and he had disguised himself while hiding among the court under heavy security, Joan miraculously found him. She walked right up to the king as if God Himself paved the way. After gaining his ear, Joan told him that she was on a divine mission that began with freeing the city of Orleans.

At first, the king thought the young girl was insane and ridiculed her, but Joan refused to give up and kept pressing him. Eventually, she convinced the king that God was with her, and he agreed to give her a brigade of soldiers to lead into battle. Maybe God moved on his heart and gave Joan divine favor. Is your head spinning yet? Are you taking all this in? The king of France gave a peasant farm girl a brigade of soldiers to lead.

While the troops were being pulled together for mission impossible, Joan took a quick lesson in military fighting and was fitted for armor. News of Joan's vision from God and the king's sanction reached Orleans before she did, causing hope to spring up in the people. That tends to happen when God's people act.

She and her men were cheered upon their entrance to the city. Joan's team and the French army brigades already present came up with a plan. The soldiers already there would create a diversion on the west side of the city, allowing Joan and her troops to storm the eastern gate, taking the English by surprise. During the heat of the battle an arrow pierced Joan's neck. She pulled it out quickly, had the wound dressed, and returned to the fight.

After the dust settled, the English were driven out and the city of Orleans was once again free. This victory led by Joan of Arc was a defining moment in the Hundred Years' War. The whole French royal army was rejuvenated and inspired. Over the next two months, Joan led the French army in several more memorable victories.

Joan of Arc's story is a historical fact.[1] To be fair, many secular historians say that she was schizophrenic to believe that God spoke to her and gave her visions. However, one can't deny that the king eventually believed her and entrusted troops to her. The entire French royal army followed her lead and was inspired.

Later, Joan was captured by England. After being convicted of bogus charges of witchcraft, she was burned alive at the stake. At the time, England was convicting genuine Christians for witchcraft because they threatened the religious government.[2] Witnesses claimed that as the flames engulfed her, Joan sang praises to God and asked for a cross to be held in front of her face as she called out to Jesus. Ultimately, Joan of Arc was exonerated of all charges and officially canonized as a saint in 1920 by the Catholic Church.

According to our beliefs, as soon as we get born again, we are all saints capable of doing what Joan did with the help of the Holy Spirit. The following is what Charles Spurgeon—known as the prince of preachers and who, by the way, was from England—had to say about Joan of Arc:

> Do not talk to me about Joan of Arc! This is the true heroine. She is battling with death, and singing while she dies. Fear? She has long forgotten what that means. Doubt? It is banished. Distress? Despondency? She has left them all behind. She is a believer; she has received Jesus, and she has power to be a child of God. Oh, the honour and dignity of being born from above![3]

It seems Charles Spurgeon believed in Joan of Arc and that is good enough for me! She was a human tsunami.[4]

A BLOOD-STAINED PLEDGE

In July 1917, during World War I, U.S. Army Private Martin August Treptow was working as a barber in Eagle Point, Wisconsin, when he stepped up to the call and enlisted in the Army. Once overseas and entrenched in battle on the Western Front, Treptow volunteered to deliver a critical message to one of his company's platoons. He understood the risk fully, and while en route was shot down by a shower of enemy bullets just as he reached the platoon commander with the message.

Afterward, when Treptow's body was recovered, a little blood-stained journal was discovered in his shirt pocket. On the front page he had painstakingly written the following words:

> America must win this war. Therefore, I will work, I will save, I will sacrifice, I will endure, I will fight cheerfully and do my utmost, as if the issue of the whole struggle depended on me alone.[5]

Just as "Remember the Alamo" had become a rallying call to the troops at the battle at San Jacinto, Martin Treptow's pledge became a rallying call in World War I. It was used on posters and pamphlets and in speeches, becoming as "effective against the enemy as a score of machine guns."[6] Sometimes a human tsunami is the quiet soul who makes a decision that affects millions but is never known.

PEANUTS ON THE PLANE

Pastor Hank Kunneman was telling us a story the other morning about how when the mask mandates were in effect on planes, he had a brilliant and humorous idea of how to be a tsunami of light. He was eating a bag of peanuts—slowly, ever so slowly. Okay, he was making them last the whole flight to avoid wearing his mask. It was *really* messing with the flight attendant. She was ready to get the pilot.

Pastor Hank proceeded to inform her that the studies done on the paper masks show that they are ineffective and don't really prevent the virus from spreading. Now there are some voices citing research that masks may actually contribute to cancer.[7] Let alone the fact that the air in the plane is recirculated from within the cabin for the entire flight. Not exactly purified air. Back to the story.

So she was extremely agitated and kept threatening to get the pilot involved. Pastor Hank questioned, would she really get the pilot involved and potentially turn the plane around because he was eating his peanuts so slowly? Isn't it funny that the virus knows not to spread if you're eating or drinking or six feet away from someone?

Then there were the people during the lockdowns who, when the churches were closed, decided to have church at Walmart or Home Depot. Because we all know that germs are only restricted to places of worship and not liquor stores or a certain DC leader's hairdresser salon or a certain West Coast governor's restaurant party.

When Seattle heard that Sean Feucht was coming to have a worship service in a northeast city park, they put chain link fences all around it. Sean decided they could walk the streets singing worship music.

Because of government's overreaching restrictions, small towns and homeowners' associations are now printing their own newspapers to connect with each other. What can you do? You can go for a walk in your community and start talking to neighbors, make your uncensored voice heard face-to-face.

We are not saying that you will be the next Joan of Arc or Private Martin Treptow. But how many people do you know who selflessly are doing what needs to be done, giving their all, making bold stands for God and country, for you, for freedom regardless of how it affects their livelihoods, their reputations, their safety? We'd call them common people and modern-day heroes and heroines. Remember, if you are here, you have a role.

Will you add your name to the list? Can you and should you be doing more? Do you feel the ground shifting under you, are you starting to move, will you be the tsunami of light working together with other lights to accomplish what is needed in this hour to turn the destruction to reconstruction?

What's your why? What will it take to turn you into a human tsunami? You know, there are some people who talk about working out and losing weight and being in shape, and there are those who are actually working out and losing weight and staying in shape. They work out whether they're in prison or at home using a couple of large bottles of water or a baby as their weights. They take the stairs at work and park far away from doors and walk in with backpacks.

Don't tell us what you can't do; tell us what can you do. Good always overcomes evil. You ask, "Then why has evil been winning?" Because too many good people have sat and done little to nothing to overcome evil with good. No more excuses.

It's going to take every one of us to turn things around. Simply by reading to this point in this book, you get it. You're not woke but awake. However, the task is daunting. But with our steadfast faith rooted in God, together we can affect the change America needs. History will reveal what we did in this critical hour.

Settle for nothing. Question everything. Demand the truth because it will set you free. Guard your heart because out of it flows every issue of life (see Proverbs 4:23). The tsunami has leveled the land, cleared the filth. It's time to rebuild. Evil was built on the sand. Let's build on the rock. "On Christ the solid rock I stand, all other ground is sinking sand."[8]

Originally from Scripture, a phrase from the Sermon on the Mount "a city setting on a hill"[9] is often quoted by politicians as "a city upon a hill."[10] Many politicians have used it in their speeches to convey a sense of patriotism needed in America.

Again, I want to quote President Ronald Reagan, this time from his speech "A Vision for America" on his election eve, November 3, 1980:

> I have quoted John Winthrop's[11] words more than once on the campaign trail this year—for I believe that Americans in 1980 are every bit as committed to that vision of a shining *city on a hill*, as were those long ago settlers...These visitors to that city on the Potomac do not come as white or black, red or yellow; they are not Jews or Christians; conservatives or liberals; or Democrats or Republicans. They are Americans awed by what has gone before, proud of what for them is still...a shining *city on a hill.*[12]

The tsunami of darkness will not win. America will not die. They cannot have us. We will push back. We will never give up. We are getting wiser, stronger, and more aware. We will take back our gates of influence and authority. We will occupy. We will overcome. We will win. Remember, we are "One nation, under God, indivisible, with liberty and justice for all."

It seems fitting to end this book with a prayer from George Washington, our first president. He understood that from the beginning our nation was in covenant with God as Robert Hunt understood in 1607 at Cape Henry. May Washington's prayer become our prayer as we march forward:

> Almighty Father, if it is thy holy will, that we shall obtain a place and name among the nations of the earth, grant that we may be enabled to show our gratitude for thy goodness, by our endeavours to fear and obey thee. Bless us with wisdom in our counsels, success in battle, and let our victories be tempered with humanity. Endow also our enemies with enlightened minds, that they become sensible of their injustice, and willing to restore our liberty and peace. Grant the petition of thy servant for the sake of Him whom thou has called thy Beloved Son; nevertheless, not my will, but thine be done.[13]

NOTES

1. "Saint Joan of Arc," *Britannica;* https://www.britannica.com/summary/Saint-Joan-of-Arc; accessed April 24, 2024.
2. "Joan of Arc: Saint or Witch," *churchinhistory.org,* March 12, 2018; http://churchinhistory.org/pages/intro-sum/saint-witch.htm; accessed April 24, 2024.
3. C.H. Spurgeon, sermon at The Metropolitan Tabernacle, January 1, 1970, *The Spurgeon Center;* https://www.spurgeon.org/resource-library/sermons/faith-and-its-attendant-privileges/#flipbook/; accessed April 24, 2024.
4. This story is from yet-to-be-published book by Zach Clinton, *Built Different.* Used by permission.
5. "PV2 Martin August Treptow," *Military Hall of Honor,* https://militaryhallofhonor.com/honoree-record.php?id=211697; accessed April 24, 2024.
6. "Pvt. Treptow's Pledge," https://www.arlingtoncemetery.net/martin-treptow.htm; accessed April 29, 2024.
7. Phillip Schneider, "Long-Term Mask Use May Contribute to Advanced Stage Lung Cancer, Study Finds," *BlacklistedNews.com,* January 29, 2021; https://www.blacklistednews.com/article/79130/longterm-mask-use-may-contribute-to-advanced-stage-lung-cancer-study.html?fbclid=IwAR1hC8uJHa-Nt31wum38uFyqiDCeWi9uhurH_26xGyjVlZ0IylM5_C5zLPQ; accessed April 24, 2024.
8. Edward Mote, "My hope is built on nothing less," hymn published 1864.
9. Patrick T. Reardon, "'As a City on a Hill': Excavating the cultural history behind a defining American phrase," *Chicago Tribune,*

May 9, 2019; https://www.chicagotribune.com/2019/01/15/as-a-city-on-a-hill-excavating-the-cultural-history-behind-a-defining-american-phrase/; accessed April 24, 2024.

10. "Shining City Upon A Hill," Matthew 5:14; https://www.openbible.info/topics/shining_city_upon_a_hill; accessed April 24, 2024.

11. John Winthrop, *Britannica,* April 16, 2024; https://www.britannica.com/biography/John-Winthrop-American-colonial-governor; accessed April 24, 2024.

12. Ronald Reagan, "Election Eve Address 'A Vision for America,'" November 3, 1980, https://www.reaganlibrary.gov/archives/speech/election-eve-address-vision-america; accessed April 24, 2024.

13. E.C. M'Guire, *The Religious Opinions and Character of Washington* (New York: Harper & Brothers, 1836), 166.

ABOUT THE AUTHORS

Together, Gene and Teri Bailey inspire thousands every day to stand up as Americans. Through the popular television program *FlashPoint*, Gene hosts a variety of guests, leaders, newsmakers and politicians each week covering current events and stories that matter.

With a background in business, childcare development and with a heart for women, Teri inspires "mama bears" globally to rise up and protect their families from a very real evil—the destruction of the family unit.

FOR MORE
RESOURCES AND
PRODUCTS VISIT:
GENEBAILEY.COM
10% OFF
CODE "B10"

In the Right Hands, This Book Will Change Lives!

Most of the people who need this message will not be looking for this book. To change their lives, you need to **put a copy of this book in their hands.**

Our ministry is constantly seeking methods to find the people who need this anointed message to change their lives. **Will you help us reach these people?**

Extend this ministry by sowing three, five, ten, or *even more* books today and change people's lives for the better! Your generosity will be part of catalyzing the Great Awakening that many have been prophesying and praying for.